REPORT WRITING

MANAGEMENT SKILL GUIDE

REPORT WRITING

Janet W. Macdonald

Croner Publications Limited
Croner House
London Road
Kingston upon Thames
Surrey KT2 6SR
Telephone: 081-547 3333

Copyright © 1992 J. W. Macdonald
First published 1992
Reprinted 1992

Published by
Croner Publications Ltd,
Croner House,
London Road,
Kingston upon Thames,
Surrey KT2 6SR
Telephone: 081-547 3333

British Library Cataloguing-in-Publication Data
A CIP Catalogue Record for this book
is available from the British Library

ISBN 1-85452-072-5

Printed in Great Britain by
Whitstable Litho Printers Ltd., Whitstable, Kent.

Contents

Chapter 1
Definitions

What are Reports?

Reports are an important part of the decision-making process in every management situation. Whether a commercial enterprise, a local or central government agency, or a public body is involved, decisions cannot be made without careful consideration of all the relevant facts.

Although facts can be presented verbally to decision makers, it is usual to present them in a written form which can be considered at length. It is this presentation of facts, which is usually accompanied by recommendations on what should be done, that is known as a report.

Reports can take many forms:

(a) simple reports in memo form
(b) pro forma reports such as:
    (i) staff appraisal reports
    (ii) accident reports
    (iii) reports on other frequently recurring situations
(c) reports comparing rival products or services
(d) reports on internal situations which could be improved
(e) reports on the findings of public enquiries
(f) other reports.

Simple reports in memo form

In an uncomplicated situation, or one where small amounts of money are involved, a memorandum is often all that is required. As long as the memo does not exceed two pages, the layout can be simple and the writing style informal. It may not even need paragraph headings as long as the main heading is clear.

Example

The stationery buyer of a large company has asked his assistant to look for a source of cheaper thermal photocopier paper.

The assistant writes as follows:

Memorandum

To: F Green
From: B Gray   23rd September

Re: Photocopier Paper

I have looked into the costs of paper as you asked.

Apart from our current suppliers, Acme, there are only two sources of treated paper: Bestpack and Chemi-bond.

As you know, Acme operate a daily delivery service. This may be why they are expensive.

Bestpack offer 10 ream boxes of white at 20 pence per ream less than Acme and colours at 35 pence per ream less. They normally deliver in this area on Fridays, but will deliver quantities of more than 200 boxes within two days of receipt of order.

Chemi-bond offer white at 10 pence per ream less than Acme. They do not stock colours but can obtain them on a week's notice. They deliver free once a week but want a 20% surcharge for short-notice delivery.

Bestpack are clearly the cheapest and I recommend that we buy from them in future.

Pro forma reports

Although superficially no more than a simple matter of filling in blank spaces on a preprinted form, these reports still require care. The fact that the events being reported occur regularly enough to merit the printing of standard forms does not mean that they are unimportant.

Appraisal reports

Staff appraisal reports form part of personnel files and will be consulted when salaries are reviewed or promotions considered. A series of consistently poor appraisal reports may even lead to that member of staff being sacked. The writer must therefore be scrupulous in selecting the terms used and avoid the temptation to use euphemisms or exaggerations.

Accident reports

Accident reports serve several purposes:

(a) fulfil legal obligations
(b) provide information for insurance claims
(c) form part of repair instructions
(d) apportion responsibility, which may lead to disciplinary action
(e) suggest remedial action
(f) provide statistical information.

The forms for accident reports are normally quite elaborate and are often designed so that relevant portions can be sent to different departments. They will all have sections for:

(a) date, time, place and, where relevant, weather conditions
(b) sketch maps of the place where the accident happened
(c) a description of the actual accident
(d) statements from the persons involved and any witnesses
(e) details of damage and injuries,

and some may have other specialised sections.

As with appraisal reports, care must be taken when choosing words to describe incidents, especially when the writer of the report was not involved in the accident. There are often so many factors to be considered that careless use of words can lead to unjust decisions.

This is the reason why newspaper reports of road accidents use the neutral "was in collision with" rather than "was struck by". It can seem incongruous to say that a pedestrian was "in collision with" a bus, but it would be wrong to suggest that the bus driver was at fault by using the term "run over" when the pedestrian may have fallen from the pavement in a drunken stupor.

Reports comparing rival products or suppliers

There are two main reasons for preparing this type of report:

(a) to aid a purchasing decision
(b) when the rivals are in competition with the writer's own organisation, to prepare a marketing strategy or product development programme.

To aid a purchasing decision

Where the relevant factors are as simple as comparison of prices between identical products, a short informal report will often suffice. But the more factors that are involved, the less easy it becomes to choose the best of the alternatives. In these situations it is necessary to produce a complex report which discusses the variations on each factor in turn before arriving at conclusions on which is the best buy. An advanced level of technical data may be needed.

Example
The fleet manager of a national sales company is considering whether to change to a different make of car and, if so, which one. Aspects that have to be considered include not only the initial purchase price, but also the cost and frequency of servicing, reliability, petrol consumption, insurance costs and resale value, as well as the merits of many other variations between makes. It may also be worth considering whether to lease rather than buy.

The style of writing and level of language used in such a report will depend on whether the purchaser involved is the writer's own organisation or a potential customer.

It is generally considered poor form actually to decry a competitor's products, but "damning with faint praise", while pointing out the superior qualities of the alternative, is a perfectly acceptable strategy. This consideration can be carried through when selecting technical data or illustrations of the rival's product.

To prepare strategy against rivals

These reports require absolute honesty about any aspects of rival products which are superior as well as details of inferior features. They will necessarily involve a high level of technical data, including, if possible, a breakdown of costs. Advertising and marketing must be considered if they are likely to alter the customer's perception of the end product. There will be many sensitive pieces of information which could mean the report has a restricted circulation. In this situation the compilation of information and the actual writing will have to be carried out in conditions of secrecy.

The writer may need to exercise considerable tact if the report reaches a conclusion that involves scrapping the chairman's pet product. In order to avoid career-damaging unpopularity, it is wise to check whether such hazards exist before wording the conclusions and making recommendations.

Reports on internal situations

Unless one is reporting on situations which are already under one's control, or by invitation from those directly involved, producing such reports is another opportunity to make enemies. Considerable tact and persuasive skills are called for if co-operation is needed to produce worthwhile results.

Situations needing such reports could be:

(a) justifying major expenditure on a new computer system
(b) altering procedures to comply with legislation
(c) rationalising staffing levels
(d) other cost-cutting exercises
(e) the introduction of a "no smoking" rule.

The justification for most of these reports is an opportunity to improve efficiency or reduce costs, but the end product will inevitably involve changing established working practices. Where trade unions are involved, any report that suggests such changes must include details of the union representative's opinions.

Reports on the findings of public enquiries

These reports are no more than accident reports or internal situation reports on a grander scale. The accidents involved are major, such as a serious train crash or industrial explosion, while the "internal situation" will relate to the functioning of an aspect of a public body's work, such as the policing of inner-city trouble spots or the teaching of science in junior schools.

The differences of scale are that the investigation of the facts will be by an appointed committee instead of an individual, and that the recommendations often involve changes in the law. Where accidents have resulted in multiple deaths or injuries, or major damage to property, the publication of the report may lead to prosecution of the responsible parties as well as claims for compensation.

As may be expected, reports on such serious matters will be presented and written with absolute formality. This does not mean that they have to be pompous or couched in legal terminology which makes them difficult to read. On the contrary, they tend to be models of readability and correct use of the English language, reducing complex situations to terms which a layman can understand, and as such are essential reading for any aspiring report writer.

Common Features

As can be seen from the above, a report is something that is produced by one person or a group of people so that another person or group of people can make a decision. In its simplest form a report can be delivered verbally, but it is more usually a formal document which details facts, reaches conclusions about those facts and makes recommendations.

Although a report can be a method of bringing a superior's attention to a situation which the writer feels needs rectifying, it is normally produced as the result of a request from above. The more elaborate the document and the more detailed the contents, the less favourable is the likely response to time having been spent on a matter which the superior may consider to be of small importance.

In such situations it is preferable to raise the subject in general terms to gauge the response before embarking on a major investigation. A simple memo saying "I believe we may be able to buy photocopier paper at better rates from a different supplier. Would you like me to investigate?" is all that is needed. This puts the report back into the category of something that has been officially requested.

The other main common feature of reports is that they are the result of investigations. It is rare that all the necessary facts can be assembled from the writer's own experience. Usually it is necessary to gather the facts from various sources and consider their relevance before starting to write.

A good report is one which contains all the information needed to allow the reader to make a good decision. It will not contain information which is incorrect or superfluous and for this reason it is usual to give details of the source of the information so that it can be checked. The information should be set out in a sequence which allows the reader to follow the logic which leads to the conclusions and recommendations.

Since reports are written to achieve a purpose, and since decision makers like their task to be simplified by reducing the number of options available, all reports end with conclusions or recommendations. Some have both, although this is less common in business reports than accident reports. Examination of the events preceding an accident will lead to the conclusion of what caused it and recommendations of how to prevent a recurrence follow from this.

Who Writes Reports?

Anyone may be called on to write a report, but the more formal types are usually written by line managers or professional specialists. The ability to write good reports is an important skill that improves the writer's career prospects and it is therefore a skill that is worth taking a little trouble to acquire.

Summary

Reports are an important part of the modern decision-making process. They come in many forms, from a single page memo to a formal printed document, but they all have common features. These include an investigation into relevant facts, conclusions drawn from examination of these facts, or recommendations as to what action or decision should follow. The ability to produce good reports is a valuable skill.

Chapter 2
Terms of Reference

If a report is to achieve its purpose, it is essential to know what that purpose is, so the report writer's first task is to achieve a precise definition. It is also necessary to define other areas, all of which can be done by asking a series of basic questions:

(a) What is the objective?
(b) What parameters are there?
(c) What authority is available?
(d) Who will the readers be?
(e) What is the time-scale?
(f) What is the budget?
(g) What resources are available?

The answers to some of these questions may prompt a further series of questions, all of which will need answering in the early stages. To avoid the unpopularity which comes from continual queries, the best approach is to produce a list of all the areas that need defining before work can commence. Experience with reports in general and the organisation in particular will enable the writer to reduce the number of subordinate questions.

What is the objective?

The success of the report is dependent on a full answer to this question.

The simple report in Chapter 1 was tightly defined: investigate cheaper sources of thermal photocopier paper. The report itself would have been more complex if there had been more suppliers and more pricing and delivery structures, but otherwise there was little more the report writer could have done without exceeding the given terms of reference.

Had the objective been the wider one of seeking ways to reduce expenditure on photocopying paper, the writer could have investigated the relative costs of thermal and plain paper, the possibilities of using a lower-quality paper for all or some copying jobs, copying on both sides of the paper instead of only one side, or requiring the machine operator to keep a detailed log of all paper used to discourage staff from copying their personal papers. Interestingly, while these ideas could well lead to less money being spent on paper, they could equally involve greater costs elsewhere.

Plain paper copiers may cost more to purchase or lease, as would machines capable of two sided copying and double paper capacity. The latter would be necessary if two grades of paper were used, unless the operator constantly changed the paper. In this case, and where the log was requested, so much time would be spent that it might be necessary to employ more staff. These suggestions would be acceptable if the report commissioner was happy for costs to move from stationery to equipment or staff budgets, but they would not do if the stated objective was to reduce the costs of photocopying.

There are a number of ways in which this might be done, starting with paper or machinery and moving through economy drives linked to profit-sharing schemes to that dream of the electronics industry, the paperless office. Electronic mail systems are the perfect way to reduce or even eliminate the photocopying budget. The snag is that they are expensive to install and maintain, involving not only hardware but the ongoing task of training staff in their use.

Once again, it has been possible to suggest ways to solve one problem by the simple method of moving it to another area. But has the problem moved in its entirety? Installing an electronic mail network for the sole purpose of eliminating photocopying is like taking a sledge-hammer to crack a nut. Tacking the same facility on to an existing or proposed computer system is comparatively cheap and entirely feasible. Saving money on photocopying has moved from being an objective on its own to being part of an even wider objective: reducing office costs.

As before, there are several ways of tackling this objective, each of which has many aspects. What could have been dealt with as a one page memo in response to a simple and tightly defined instruction has grown to a multi-sectioned and probably multi-paged document. It should not take long to think of all the areas that could be investigated and written up. Closely following those thoughts will come the reflection that there is also a one line answer to the question of how to reduce office costs: close the office!

This bald suggestion, although it may be the ultimate solution to the problem, is not likely to endear the writer to higher authority, since it smacks of an inability to recognise the gravity of the task. On the other hand, the opposite extreme of a long rambling report covering all possible aspects in copious and minute detail could be interpreted as an inability to focus on the essentials.

At this point it is worth mentioning that the report writer also has an objective. This might include the ulterior motive of demonstrating such personal brilliance that a promotion will follow, but it is quite simply to produce a report that helps the person who asked for it to meet his or her objective.

Rather like putting blinkers on a horse, these interlinked objectives are best achieved by eliminating irrelevant distractions. This requires definition of the term "relevant", otherwise known as setting parameters.

What parameters are there?

The first area that must be clarified is the importance of achieving the objective which the report is addressing. Does it matter more than anything else? Does it matter more than some things and less than others? If so, where does it fit in the chain of importance? Or is it merely something which would be nice to achieve, but does not really matter?

To return to the objective of reducing office costs, it is first necessary to define the purpose of that office. Is it essential to the enterprise's survival? This heading covers functions as diverse as compliance monitoring in an investment company or the cashiers in a department store. The Financial Services Act 1986 demands the presence of compliance staff as a condition of trading. Current payment methods require people to count and bank money in a way that satisfies auditors, VAT and Inland Revenue officials, but credit cards, bank debit cards and modern electronic point of sale equipment are rapidly rendering cash and cheques obsolete. The human beings who account for these transactions may soon be unnecessary.

If the office is not a legal requirement, is it commercially essential? This category covers all the ramifications of the tasks of accepting and processing orders, producing and handling goods, demanding and handling payments.

Clearly, reducing costs in the areas that are legally or commercially essential can only be done by increasing efficiency or reducing the costs of physically running the offices. (This might involve seeking cheaper sources of supplies or relocation to cheaper premises.)

What cannot be considered is reducing the quality of service given by these departments. There are areas where this might be tolerable, such as a complaints department, where personal letters to disgruntled customers could be superseded by an all-purpose postcard or credit voucher. But if the public image of the company, and therefore its essential loyal customer base, is dependent on maintaining a friendly reputation, such departments join the list of absolute essentials.

In this case, the objective has become more definite: to reduce office costs without damaging the company's reputation for service.

The next area for definition is the time-scale set for achieving the objective. This month? Next year? In ten years? In the office situation, a few weeks allows for little more than finding discount suppliers, several months permits interdepartmental reorganisations and redundancy programmes, and ten years is plenty of time to find a site to build a new fully automated factory and office complex which requires no more staff than a few button pressers.

The final areas that require clarification are the actual words used. "Reduce" is a very vague term which could easily be wrongly interpreted unless the following questions are asked:

(a) By what percentage should costs be reduced?
(b) As a percentage of what – last year's costs, this year's budgeted figure or a proportion of income?
(c) Should they be reduced permanently or temporarily; if temporarily, for how long?

When these questions, and any others that come to mind, have been answered, it is possible to produce a precise objective: eg to reduce office costs by 25 per cent over the next five years without damaging the company's reputation for service.

Scope

In some ways scope could be considered to be another parameter, but since it indicates levels of magnitude it should be considered separately. This is particularly important when a problem stems from deep-seated causes rather than exceptional events, for the report may need to apportion blame and suggest preventive measures as well as ways to alleviate the effect.

A desire to reduce office costs implies an admission that they are currently excessive. In a recession, this may be a simple matter of insufficient income to support the expenditure, but in other economic climates it could involve extravagance or lack of control. In other words, someone is failing to do their job properly.

Discovering who that person is and whether their failure is due to lack of guidance, incompetence, or a desire to line their pockets with bribes from high-priced suppliers, adds another dimension to the report. There are further dimensions beyond this one, such as a need to introduce a better staff selection system, or overhaul internal audit procedures, all of which would widen the scope of the report.

Authority

The wider the scope of the report, the more essential is the need for good authority for the necessary investigations. Some organisations are rigidly territorial and the holder of each territory will defend it strenuously against "intruders". Since people's main concern is usually fear that they will be exposed as incompetent or unnecessary, they tend to view attempts to win their co-operation with suspicion. In such situations it may be necessary to threaten them.

This could be done by suggesting that the report will label them obstructionist, but since actually carrying out this threat is a tacit admission of failure by the writer, it is far better to forestall such problems by defining the authorisation at the start.

How this is actually done will depend on the organisation. In some, a simple memo or telephone call saying "I have been asked by the chairman . . . " will suffice, while in others it may be necessary for the memo to come direct from the chairman. For the highest-level reports it may be necessary for authorisation to be given at a minuted board meeting, while in some government departments or nationalised industries the writer will need a categorised security clearance.

It is essential to have this authority well established before any investigations can begin, particularly when the writer is new to the organisation and most likely to cause offence by treading on what everyone else knows to be super-sensitive toes.

Who will the readers be?

Although not necessarily the first question to be asked, this is one of the most important, as the answer will determine the structure and tone of the report. There may be only one reader, or several, in different layers of importance:

(a) a principal decision maker
(b) subsidiary decision makers or decision influencers
(c) people who do not take part in the decision process but who need the information contained in the report
(d) historians.

Principal decision maker

This tends to be the person who controls expenditure, whether in the writer's organisation or as an outside organisation. This might be a customer or the person who allocates grant funding and since their criteria for making decisions could be diametrically opposed, it is necessary to know quite a lot about them, including:

(a) what does that person already know about the subject of the report?
(b) what does that person want to know?
(c) apart from using it to make the decision, what other use will be made of the information?
(d) does this mean any information should be held back?
(e) does the decision maker have personal expertise, or will other experts be called in?
(f) are pure facts required or will educated opinions be accepted or even preferred?
(g) are there any cultural differences between the writer and the decision maker which the former should be aware of ? These might be any of the classic areas of misunderstanding, from nationality and race, through social class and religion to gender
(h) are there any other areas of prejudice or enthusiasm which the writer should be aware of ?

Subsidiary decision makers or influencers

These might be members of a board of directors or executive committee, or technical experts called in to verify the accuracy and relevance of technical information.

All the questions asked about the principal should also be asked about these people, then a few other questions are needed, including:

14

(a) do any of them hold views which will cause them vehemently to oppose the decision recommended by the report?
(b) do any of them have personal or professional prejudices against the report writer?
(c) will the principal decision maker be irrationally influenced by these people?

People who need the information

The main considerations here are the level of information needed and whether providing any of this information will breach confidentiality. This does not mean that what they need should be withheld from them, but that the report should be structured in such a way that confidential information can be removed before the rest is circulated. The easiest way of doing this is by the judicious use of appendices.

If the information users require more depth of data than the decision makers, they could be given copies of the source data as well as the appendices to the report.

Historians

This is a blanket term, used here to cover all the people who might have occasion to refer to the report without being directly affected by its content. They could be journalists, archivists, students or the general public. Obviously not all reports are available to such people and the writer should not consider their opinion if it conflicts with the defined objective, but where access is unlimited it might be necessary to provide a glossary of technical terms.

What is the time-scale?

This is not the time-scale in which the objectives will be achieved, but the time allotted for completion of the report itself. Since most reports are required for a specific purpose, it follows that they will be needed at a particular time and it is rare that the delivery date will be left open.

It is essential that the writer should know when completion is required and if it is possible tactfully to insist on verification of that date it is wise to do so. There can be few things more irritating than to skimp on details to meet a deadline only to find that the recipient is on holiday or embroiled in other activities which leave the report untouched in an in-tray for days.

Obviously the greater the scope of the report and the more complex its structure, the longer it will take to produce. Only experience will allow the writer to assess the time needed for each stage and even an experienced writer knows that an additional margin of time should be added to allow for inevitable delays. This luxury is only available if the writer is allowed to set the completion date. In most cases that date has already been set and the writer must plan how best to use the time available.

There are several steps that apply to all reports:

(a) deciding what information is needed
(b) gathering the information
(c) sorting the information
(d) deciding on the format
(e) writing the first draft
(f) rewriting for the final version
(g) reproduction
(h) distribution.

Some reports may have to be circulated at the first draft stage for comments which will have to be incorporated into the final version. This final version may have to be approved by a superior before it can be reproduced and distributed.

These various stages constitute a series of mini-deadlines and it is possible to draw up a schedule of dates to meet them. The most easily measured time-scales are those at the end and it should be possible to allocate a specific number of days to each stage, thus:

– The report is to be discussed at the board meeting on 21 June.
– Items for discussion at board meetings must be circulated to board members seven days before the meeting, so the final printed report must be with the managing director's secretary by 13 June.
– Reprographics department requires three days to print, collate and bind, so the approved version must be with them by 10 June.
– The writer's superior wants two days to read the final draft and may require changes. Allow seven days in all – 5 June.
– The typist needs two days to make alterations after the first draft has been circulated. Writing the changes takes, say, two days – 1 June.
– Allow two weeks for comments on the first draft, so distribute it by 18 May.

The date is now 4 March, so ten weeks are available to gather and sort the information, chase any missing information, write the first draft and produce any illustrations needed. Allocating four weeks to writing and four weeks to gathering information leaves two weeks for sorting and chasing missing information.

What is the budget?

A comparatively simple report, which requires no travelling or extra staff to collect information, no special illustrations, and which can be typed and printed in-house will not necessarily need an allocated budget. A major report which needs to be completed quickly and printed in full colour with professional photographs will cost more than can be easily absorbed in the writer's normal departmental running costs. If extra costs are involved, the writer will need to produce some costings for approval unless a special budget already exists.

Areas which could involve extra expenditure will include:

(a) travel and entertainment relating to the collection of information
(b) purchase of reference material
(c) fees to researchers, consultants or temporary staff
(d) fees to photographers or illustrators
(e) fees for use of copyright material
(f) the cost of printing, binding and distribution.

What resources are available?

This question is tied to the previous one. If a major report has a tight deadline or requires technical expertise greater than the writer's own, it will be necessary to enlist some assistance. It is often possible to borrow this assistance from other departments, thus avoiding the necessity of hiring expensive temporary staff or consultants. The writer should always take the trouble to enquire what skills are already available inside the organisation, having first checked on who has responsibility for the various tasks after the actual writing is complete. These tasks include:

(a) proof-reading
(b) collating the typescript and illustrations
(c) production of illustrations
(d) page numbering
(e) taking the typescript (or coded PC disk) to the printers
(f) producing the distribution list.

Summary

In order to produce a report that achieves its purpose, it is necessary to define the terms of reference. These will include not only a precise definition of the objective and scope of the report, but also give the writer an insight into the recipients of the report that will allow the structure and tone to be focused for that particular audience. Also included in these terms of reference are the essential pieces of information on completion date, what help is available and how much may be spent on producing the report, as well as the provision of the necessary authority to get the job done.

Chapter 3
Collecting and Organising Information

Since a report consists of a sequence of information which is presented in a logical order so that conclusions can be reached, it follows that the writer must begin by collecting information. Although at first thought it seems a simple enough task to gather and record various facts and opinions, if this job is not approached in a disciplined manner, the later goal of bringing the report together in a coherent form will be much more difficult.

Acknowledgement of Sources

Unless the writer has been selected as an accredited expert in the subject of the report, information will have to be gathered from outside sources. It is usual to acknowledge these sources for two reasons:

1. Where the information has come from an individual or an organisation, it is polite to do so and will ensure future co-operation if it is needed.
2. It lends veracity and authority to the facts and opinions selected for inclusion in the final draft and allows interested parties to pursue specific aspects if they wish.

Where the source is a previously published document, the acknowledgement is normally in the form of references. These are dealt with in more detail in Chapter 4, but usually consist of a reference number in the text and full details of the document given as a footnote or in an appendix.

Where an individual or organisation is concerned, the normal method is to have a section headed "acknowledgements" at the beginning. It can be difficult, when several people have helped, to select the order in which to mention them without giving offence to those who are not at the top of the list, so unless a clear order of social or professional precedence exists, it is safest to list them in alphabetical order of surname. There are alternatives, such as by subject matter or in the same order as the section to which they contributed.

The qualifications of each individual or the basis of their expertise should always be given. There are several ways in which this can be done:

(a) F. Bloggs FCII, Senior Manager, Pensions Department, Acme Insurance plc

(b) F. Bloggs, author of "Pensions Planning for Wheel Tappers and Shunters"

(c) Professor F. Bloggs, Cantab, Head of Insurance Studies, University of Croydon

(d) Fred Bloggs, Founder and past Chairman of the National Association of Wheeltappers and Shunters.

There should be a clear indication of the nature of the contribution and, in particular, whether it is in the form of fact or opinion. Some useful phrases in this connection are:

(a) for the benefit of his opinion on . . .

(b) for allowing quotations from his book . . .

(c) for allowing access to case studies of . . .

(d) for providing statistics on . . .

In order to give credit where it is due, each piece of information should include details of its source so that there can be no confusion later. Where there are several items from the same source, it may be convenient to use a cross-referencing system.

Some contributors may prefer to remain anonymous and this fact should be clearly noted at the head of whatever data storage system is used. Where the report is confidential it may be preferable to disguise the identity of

the source by the use of a code-name.
It is unforgivable to misspell a source's name.

Research Techniques

There are many sources of information, all useful in the appropriate context:

(a) libraries and computer data-bases
(b) chambers of commerce and trade associations
(c) professional associations
(d) educational facilities
(e) personal contacts
(f) skilled researchers
(g) company marketing departments
(h) credit reference agencies or commercial investigators
(i) internal reports and returns
(j) other internal documents.

Libraries

As well as public libraries, where an enormous diversity of information is available, there are many other libraries and computer databases with varying degrees of specialisation. If approached in an appropriate way, most are extremely helpful and willing to provide information. Some may charge a small fee for photocopying and postage. These libraries can be located through the reference sections of public libraries and may be found at:

(a) colleges, universities and museums
(b) industrial training boards
(c) professional associations
(d) charitable organisations
(e) commercial organisations, especially large companies with training departments
(f) newspapers and periodicals.

Chambers of commerce and trade associations

As well as having libraries, these organisations usually have a public relations consultant who will be delighted to send information or suggest useful contacts. They rarely charge for this service.

Professional associations

While these bodies may not be enthusiastic about allowing non-members to have access to their libraries, the secretary will usually suggest some expert members to give opinions. These members will probably be Fellows and will require a fee.

Educational facilities

Some facilities restrict their libraries to students, but most are helpful to outsiders, provided it is not exam time. They will have copies of papers relating to the subjects they teach, as well as a comprehensive selection of books on those subjects. The facility's general office will pass enquiries on to the relevant head of department (who will also be preoccupied at exam time).

Personal contacts

The writer's contacts will have contacts of their own and some persistent telephoning, together with judicious applications of lunch, will often bring forth the desired information.

Skilled researchers

Professional researchers are available in many fields, and can be found through their advertisements in relevant journals. They usually charge for their services on a time-plus-expenses basis, but can safely be left to do the job to an agreed deadline. They will need a precisely defined brief to work to, and will, if desired, provide referees to vouch for their integrity in confidential matters.

A cheaper source of research is postgraduates who are filling in time before taking jobs.

Company marketing departments

Marketing departments will produce copious quantities of information about their products, and will probably continue to do so long after the report is complete and the purchasing decision has been made in another company's favour. The literature they send will, of course, be biased, but may well contain nuggets of information that lead the writer into previously unconsidered areas of research.

If many companies supply similar items or services, a check-list of desired features will allow some preliminary weeding out.

Credit reference agencies or commercial investigators

These sources of information used only to be employed by credit granters. In the current climate of mergers and business collapses it has become necessary to carry out deep investigations into essential suppliers, potential partners or predators, and even senior members of staff.

The best firms are those which specialise in various areas of commerce or industry. They rarely advertise, so can only be located by word of mouth, and will neither disclose their own sources of information nor wish to be identified in the report themselves.

If given a wide enough brief, they will often provide the answers to questions which nobody had thought to ask, so it is best to give them as free a hand as time and the budget will allow.

Internal reports, returns and other documents

Most matters relating to the internal running of any organisation are the subjects of regular reports or returns. Some departments, notably sales or marketing, publish these returns. Since sales people tend to prefer looking to the future, it is not always easy to obtain copies of historical returns, but there is usually someone who keeps copies of everything.

Prising such information out of internal audit, management accounts or heads of other departments may require high-level authority.

Interviewing and Other Techniques

While basic research techniques will provide all the information needed for many reports, there are certain types of report which require fieldwork or technical investigations. Fieldwork can include questionnaires, which have to be carefully worded if the answers are not to produce worthless results, but more usually involves interviews.

Interviewing

The purpose of conducting an interview is to uncover facts and opinions which might not otherwise be forthcoming because the person involved:

(a) does not think they are relevant
(b) is not literate enough to write them accurately
(c) does not wish to disclose them
(d) is physically incapable of writing as a result of injury.

Details considered to be irrelevant

This is a situation which requires patience and often more than one interview. Although the golden rule for interviews is to ask "open" questions, the interviewer who believes there may be more to disclose can formulate these questions in such a way that they are finely directed.

Where witnesses have stated that they saw the bus pass over the pedestrian but did not see it actually knock him down because they were looking the other way at that moment, it might be worth asking why they were looking away. The question "Did you notice anything about the pedestrian when he approached the bus-stop?" is still open, but should produce quite a detailed answer.

Some of the content of that answer may be subjective. People who are themselves regular heavy drinkers may say "Oh, he'd had a few, he was a bit unsteady on his feet", whereas a lifelong teetotaller would say "He was in a disgusting state, stinking of beer and staggering all over the pavement".

Whatever the response, it is necessary to persist until a clear picture is obtained.

Non-literate witnesses

The fact that witnesses are not adept at writing down what they saw or heard does not necessarily mean they are actually illiterate or stupid, and the interviewer must take care not to convey this assumption. The interviewer's task here is to guide the witness through the incident in a logical fashion, recording the answers verbatim. If these verbatim answers are too obscure for lay readers to follow, it may be necessary to seek clarification with some "Do you mean . . . ?" questions. Even obscenities should be recorded verbatim, although they may need to be edited out of the published report.

Uncooperative or hostile witnesses

There are four reasons why witnesses may not be prepared to disclose what they know:

(a) they do not want to be called to give evidence in court
(b) they feel they might get someone (including themselves) into trouble
(c) they object to the interviewer's manner
(d) they have a general hostility to any form of authority.

Whatever the motivation, unless the interviewer is in a position to insist on answers to direct questions, it may be impossible to do more than record a suspicion that the witnesses knew more than they would tell.

Injured witnesses or victims

Where the interviewee is able to talk, the usual technique of open questions should be used. Otherwise it will be necessary to devise a series of questions that can be answered either "yes" or "no" by some agreed signal. Depending on the seriousness of the enquiry, an assistant may be needed to verify the responses.

Loaded questions

The purpose of conducting interviews is to ascertain the truth, not to put words into witnesses' mouths. There may not be a deliberate attempt to slant the responses, but it still tends to happen. For this reason loaded questions should be avoided, especially those which the interviewee may interpret as aggressive. The worst example is questions that start "Don't you think . . ."

Technical investigations

These will include:

(a) equipment testing
(b) laboratory experiments
(c) forensic investigations.

They are normally carried out on a formal basis by outside bodies who will produce their own report on their findings in a standardised format. Some reports will require several types of technical investigation, the results of which will then have to be collated and summarised.

Accident reports

The data in these reports will include formal documentation of technical investigations, often with diagrams and photographs; and also:

(a) formal witness statements, which should be conducted as soon as possible after the event, while details are fresh in people's memories
(b) details of the site
(c) prevailing conditions
(d) sketch maps showing the site and the position of witnesses and persons involved.

Formal witness statements

These should include:

(a) full name
(b) full address
(c) occupation
(d) any qualification which makes the statement especially valuable
(e) position during the incident
(f) times of arrival and departure from the scene.

Details of the site

As well as the map, there are many details relating to accident sites which could be relevant. These might include:

(a) details of previous accidents
(b) details of any planning applications
(c) history of civil unrest
(d) work scheduled, in progress or recently completed
(e) physical features which cannot conveniently be shown on a map.

In listing these details it is usual to progress from the permanent to the impermanent and from natural to man-made features. Permanent features would include a tree and a bridge, impermanent features would include a seasonal flood and a passing bus.

Prevailing conditions

This term refers to weather, visibility and the effects of pollution. All could be of a semi-permanent or temporary nature. High winds can be caused by topography as well as passing hurricanes, the most brilliant artificial light can be blacked out by a power cut and straw burning can send thick smoke on to a motorway. Where road traffic accidents are concerned, the state of the road itself should be given.

Sketch maps

It may be necessary to produce several maps in increasing scale, showing first the general area and then the actual site of the accident. North should be shown and an indication of well-known features or places, eg "Maidstone 6 miles".

Maps depicting the inside of buildings should show main and subsidiary entrances and stairs or lifts as well as other relevant features. Maps of outside sites should show road names and, if appropriate, traffic-flow systems and the position of vehicles. The positions of casualties and witnesses should be marked.

All maps should include a note of the scale used and precise measurements of any relevant features. The first draft of any map should be drawn on site.

Storage of Information

There are many methods of recording and storing information, ranging from bound notebooks to computer disks. The method used is a matter of personal taste, but if more than one person is collecting the information there must be agreement on a common form. Where there are copious amounts of information which will have to be sorted and organised, it is sensible to record them in a form that can easily be manipulated into order. For this reason, many experienced writers prefer to use index cards, which can be sorted and re-sorted as often as needed.

Preliminary Organisation

Information should be stored under preliminary headings from the beginning, as this makes the final sorting easier. It does not matter if the chosen headings are not the final ones, as long as they are not too far away from the prime objective. The purpose of these preliminary headings is to keep track of the amount of information that is coming in and to see whether any aspects are upsetting the overall balance.

There is nothing sacrosanct about pieces of information. The mere fact that they have been collected does not mean they have to be used if they do not add anything new to the picture. They may have some statistical value, but otherwise there is a danger of creating an irrelevant bias or, even worse, boring the reader.

Some writers make a list of the preliminary categories and sort them into order by giving each point a number, or by linking connected points with arrows. The problem with this method is that the linking arrows can get tangled, or the numbers keep getting changed round. This is where index cards are useful, as they can be moved from pile to pile without the need for an eraser or correcting fluid.

Another method of organising topics, and showing where an imbalance calls for further research, is to construct a spider diagram (see Figure 1). Also known as spray notes, scatter notes, or brain maps, these diagrams are an excellent way of linking ideas or pieces of information in a free-form way. The problem with a normal linear list is that the first item written down may not be the most important, but it is difficult to remember this when it is at the top of the list.

To construct a spider diagram, a key idea is written in the middle of a blank piece of paper and a ring is drawn round it. Other, connected ideas are written round the key idea in random order, rings are drawn round them, and each subsidiary idea is joined to the key idea with a line. Further thoughts or facts are connected to the subsidiary ideas by further rings and lines. Each new item that occurs is added in the appropriate place, building up a free-form pattern of thought or facts radiating outwards from the key idea. When nothing more can be added, the diagram is redrawn to provide a more logical progression.

Spider diagrams can seem odd to those who have not used them before, but a little perseverance will prove their value as a way of recording what is known, what still needs to be found out and even where to look for information.

Evaluation

When sufficient information has been collected, it will be necessary to

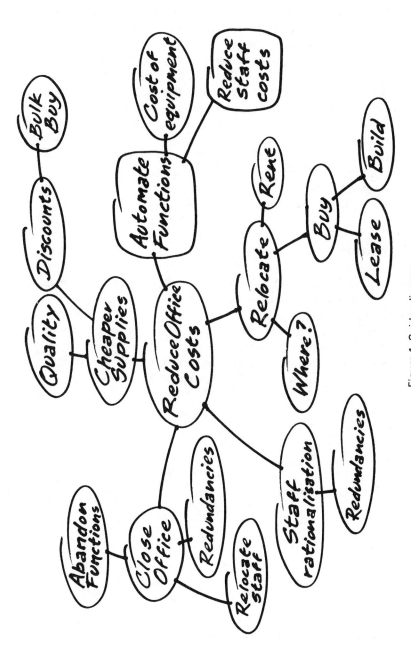

Figure 1. Spider diagram

evaluate its usefulness and accuracy. At this stage the writer should turn again to the stated objective of the report and the terms of reference, and measure each item against these crucial factors. Any items that will not serve to further the objective, or that are outside the terms of reference, must be rejected, no matter how dear they are to the writer's heart. Pure objectivity may be difficult to achieve, but there is a dividing line between subjectivity and prejudice which must not be crossed.

It is the readers who must be enlightened or convinced and both the content and the sequence of the pieces of information used must be organised to help them. Whether the sequence is in ascending or descending order of importance, price or chronology, or moves from the general to the particular, before any information is used in the first draft it must be checked again in case it is misleading, inaccurate or out of date.

Summary

Information for reports should be collected in a disciplined manner, with details of each source so that it can be acknowledged. Information can be obtained by research from various sources and individuals, by interviewing or by technical investigation. Accident reports will need statements from casualties and witnesses, as well as maps and other details relating to the site. Preliminary organisation and evaluation will show whether or not more information is needed before writing can begin.

Chapter 4
Format

Once all the necessary information has been collected and organised into preliminary groupings, the writer needs to decide what format to use before the actual writing can be done. The best structure is one that makes it easy for all levels of reader to extract as much or as little as they need.

The simplest structure has three parts:

(a) an introduction
(b) the main body of information
(c) a conclusion drawn from this information.

This format is only suitable for short reports, as otherwise the main body becomes cumbersome and difficult to use. People who receive reports fall into two categories:

(a) the few who are prepared to start at the beginning and read all the way through to the end
(b) the majority who want to dip in and select the pieces that interest them.

If the report is to be effective, it must be designed so that the majority can easily identify the sections they want. This means a more complex structure, with a contents list, subsections and appendices as well as the three sections shown above.

The full list of possible sections is as follows:

(a) title page
(b) list of contents
(c) acknowledgements
(d) terms of reference
(e) executive summary
(f) introduction
(g) foreword
(h) main text
(i) minority report
(j) conclusions
(k) recommendations
(l) appendices
(m) references
(n) bibliography
(o) glossary
(p) index
(q) distribution list.

Some of these sections may have alternative names.

The writer may be at liberty to use whichever of these seems appropriate, or may be in an organisation that has a specified format. Where there is not an approved format, the writer may want to evolve a standard one in the interests of uniformity. This is particularly useful where a report is to be produced on a routine basis, as some aspects may be used for comparison.

Title page

The title page should create a good impression because it is the first thing the reader sees. To avoid a cluttered look, it should include no more than four items – usually:

(a) the title and the fact that it is a report
(b) the name of the writer or writers
(c) if it is not the final version, the number of the draft
(d) the date when it was issued.

The title

The title of the report should be carefully worded. The English language has such flexibility that it offers constant opportunities for confusion or unintended jokes. Such words as "cutting" or "breakdown" are particularly dangerous – "cutting materials in the workshop" could refer to an after-hours dressmaking class instead of a cost-reduction exercise.

Intentional jokes are even worse. Rather like the twee names fashionable among hairdressers' salons, what seemed very witty at one time rapidly becomes so embarrassing that no one wants to be associated with it.

Titles in the form of questions should also be avoided as they tend to beg a sharp answer from the office wag. They are also redolent of the advertisements in free local newspapers.

There is no reason why a title should not be split into a brief main title and a longer, more explanatory, subtitle. This is often done with reports compiled by public committees and makes it much easier to identify the report. Whether spoken, written or filed on a computer, two or three words are easier to deal with than 20. Where the title is split in this way, the subtitle can begin "A report on . . .". Shorter titles should be followed by the words "A report by . . .".

The name of the writer

A sole writer's name should be prominently displayed immediately after the title, on a separate line. Where there are several writers involved they can be listed on the title page in whatever order the organisation's etiquette requires. However, if there are more than four or five writers, this list is better presented on a separate sheet. Where a committee has prepared a report, the "by-line" on the title page should state the name of the committee, and the members of that committee should be shown on a separate page, starting with the chairman.

The number of the draft

This is only necessary with preliminary versions and is normally shown as the two words "(Number) draft" in a corner of the title page. An alternative position is within brackets immediately after the title.

The date

This should be the date on which the report, whether a final version or an earlier draft, left the writer's hands. Any changes to the content which are made after that date cannot be considered to be the writer's responsibility and for this reason the writer should ensure that all reports are prominently dated. Dating a report also puts it in its proper place in the historical record.

List of contents

In its simplest form, the list of contents will consist of as many of the possible sections given above as are applicable. Where the main text is concerned, it will need to be shown under a heading that describes its content, unless it is very long and complex. In this case the headings of the various subsections should be shown.

Reports which include an index will need less detail in the list of contents than those which do not.

Acknowledgements

As discussed in Chapter 2, help from outside individuals and organisations should be acknowledged, with details of their qualifications to give authority to their contributions.

These acknowledgements should be kept on a business-like level, not allowed to degenerate into a page of fulsome thanks to everyone who gave the writer a cup of coffee.

Terms of reference

Where the terms of reference are straightforward or can be expressed in a short sentence, they can be stated in the subtitle or as part of the introduction rather than as a section on their own. Otherwise they should appear on a separate page, organised into their order of importance and subdivided where necessary. This task should be done before any writing of the main body of the report starts and they should be kept where they can be referred to whenever needed.

Executive summary

Busy decision makers usually want to be able to grasp the point of a report without having to wade through the whole thing. They will become impatient if a summary is not provided and may not bother to read the report at all.

The summary should consist of one page and never be more than two pages. In a complex report it will consist of a series of brief summaries of the main sections, which should be written after those sections are compiled, not before. Doing this often shows up any faults in the logic, or areas that need more detail, and it eliminates the danger of tailoring the report to the summary rather than the other way round.

Introduction

The purpose of an introduction is to describe why the report was commissioned. If this is covered in the title or subtitle, there is no need for an introduction, but the background to most situations is more complex than can be dealt with in a single sentence. Following the background, which will usually be expressed as the reason for the report, will be a brief description of the aims and the terms of reference if these have not been stated separately. Where recommendations will be made, it is usual to mention this fact at the end of the introduction.

In some cases it may be appropriate to give some details of how information was gathered and what limitations, if any, were imposed. Again, a brief mention is all that is needed rather than a full statement of the parameters.

Foreword

Forewords tend to be written by someone other than the writer of the main text. This is usually someone in a senior position who feels they should be represented, and although the writer will not be able to omit such a foreword, it may be necessary to apply some subtle editing to tone down irrelevancies or pomposity.

Forewords can add some authority to the report, but in general they serve only to distract the reader's attention.

Main text

This is the most important part of the report and it must be organised in such a way that it is both inviting and easy to read. It should fall naturally into main themes and supporting sub-themes, arranged in a pattern that leads to logical conclusions, and it should be clear from the heading chosen for each theme what is to be found in the text. As with the title of the report, words that have alternative meanings should be avoided.

Where a great deal of disparate information has been gathered, or where a technical or laboratory process is involved, there may need to be a separate section headed "Procedures" or "Methods and materials". This section would be followed by another with detailed test results and yet another to discuss those results and their implications. Even a non-technical report might need a discussion of the writer's own results when considered against other similar studies.

All these headings should be shown in the list of contents.

Minority reports

Where a report has been written by a committee, or as a result of a committee's enquiries, there may be some members who disagree with the majority opinion. In this case a minority report must be included, immediately after the rest of the main text.

It should be clearly shown in the list of contents and mentioned in any introduction or foreword. It could be the reason for the foreword, but in this case reference should only be in the form of a statement that unanimous agreement could not be reached and thus a minority report has been included.

It should be written under the same terms of reference and within the same parameters as the rest of the report. It should not contain any criticism of the majority opinion or of those who hold that opinion.

Unless the names of those who hold the minority opinion have been mentioned in the foreword, they should be shown at the beginning of the minority report.

The need for a minority report could arise for various reasons, such as:

(a) a difference in political outlook, resulting in objections to the conclusions or recommendations
(b) a difference of opinion over the interpretation of test results
(c) a feeling that the investigation did not uncover all the relevant facts.

Conclusions and recommendations

These are discussed in detail in Chapter 7.

Appendices

Also known as attachments, annexes or exhibits, appendices allow the writer to cater for all levels of reader. Most readers will be happy enough to accept the writer's précis of technical data or other detailed information, but specialists and pedants will want to see the details in full.

The best place for these details is in a separate area where they will not interfere with the main flow of the report. If there are different tranches of detailed information, they should be separated into subject headings of their own and each shown as a different appendix.

Appendices can be used for statistics, detailed results of technical tests, copies of contracts and many other items. They should not be used for graphs, charts or maps which need to be referred to when reading the main text, unless they are physically bound into the report in such a way that they can be unfolded to be visible alongside the text. This can be useful when the same item is referred to in several different places.

Appendices can be referred to in the text in a number of ways:

(a) "(see Appendix A)"
(b) "detailed results are shown in Appendix B"
(c) "the conditions under which these opacities build up are described in Appendix C".

It is normal for appendices to be designated by letters rather than numbers. They can, however, be subdivided by using numbers after the letters, eg A1, A2, A3. Although the usual sequence is A, B, C, D and so on, occasionally they will be designated by the capital letter of the main heading where they are mentioned.

Under this system, a report with the three sections "Convention qualification", "Managers' bonuses" and "Production targets" would have appendices C, M and P. This system is rather confusing and it should be avoided unless it is an approved organisational practice, especially when there are two unconnected headings beginning with the same letter and they have to be designated M1 and M2.

References

This is a list of all books, papers or unpublished work such as letters, which have been specifically referred to or quoted from in the text. It is shown in the order in which items were referred to and each entry should show the title and author; then, if it is a book, the published edition number and date on which that edition was published, followed by the name of the publishers. If it is an article in a journal or periodical, the title of the article and the author should be given, followed by the title of the journal, the volume number, issue number and page number. If it is an unpublished paper or letter, the title of the paper and the date when it was written or the date of the letter and an indication of the addressee should be given.

As soon as it becomes apparent that references will be needed, the writer should record the necessary details so that they can be slotted into place during writing. The easiest way to do this is on file cards, which can also be used to indicate whether permission has been given for quotations. It is the writer's responsibility to obtain these permissions. Failure to obtain permission may be an infringement of copyright.

There are various ways of showing references in the text. Where there are only a few, asterisks can be used with footnotes giving the details, and the list can be omitted. Otherwise numbers are used, either surmounting the text, thus[2], but sometimes in square brackets after the word, thus [2].

Bibliography

This is a list of published items which have not been specifically referred to in the text, but which have proved valuable to the writer and will enlighten the reader. It is sometimes headed "Further reading " instead of "Bibliography".

The items in a bibliography are listed in alphabetical order of the author's surname and should give the same details as in a reference list, so that copies can be found in a library or bookshop. When there is a list of references and a bibliography, it is customary to list the references first.

Glossary

A glossary becomes necessary when a technical report, which of necessity uses technical terms, will be read by the general public or members of staff such as accountants, whose own area of expertise does not require a technical vocabulary. It is also useful where verbatim witness statements have used localised slang or where a word has a different meaning in a technical context to that in the everyday world, eg "strangeness" as a property of particles in nuclear physics.

Index

It should not be necessary to have an index unless the report is very long and complex with much cross-referencing between various sections and appendices. In general, the organisation of the main body of the report should avoid these cross-references and sufficient subheadings listed in the table of contents should render an index unnecessary.

Where an index is needed, it should be prepared by the writer, who is the best judge of whether items should be included.

Distribution list

Some report writers favour putting the distribution list on the title page. Provided the list consists of no more than six names or designations such as "directors and senior managers" this is tolerable. More than six names will clutter up the title page unacceptably and thus should be listed on a separate sheet of paper bound into the report, or on a separate memo.

Footnotes

Footnotes distract the reader. In a short report, where a glossary or reference list containing only two or three items would be risible, they may be unavoidable. In general, footnotes are considered the mark of an amateur writer, as rephrasing usually renders them unnecessary.

Summary

Reports need to be structured in a format which makes it easy for all levels of reader to extract what they need. Short reports can be divided into as little as three sections, while long and complex reports may need numerous sections and appendices, together with a list of contents to show what the sections contain. Some organisations lay down the format for their reports but in most cases it is left to the writer to decide what is most suitable.

Chapter 5
Illustrations

The report writer often finds that words are not the ideal tool to convey some types of information. Of course, if enough words are used, the message can be got across, but only in a way that wastes time, space, and is frequently confusing to the reader.

Numerical Data

Where numerical data is concerned, it is especially confusing if more than two or three sets of numbers are presented in a prose sentence that stretches along a line. Such sentences should always be rewritten so that each figure starts a phrase on a new line.

Example
This month, 361 widgets per day were made by 23 machinists, which averages out at 16 each.

This month,
    23 machinists produced
    361 widgets per day, or an average
    16 widgets each.

Even this simple example of three sets of figures is easier to read when it is set out vertically instead of horizontally. Multiply the situation by adding more months and the horizontal version becomes much more difficult to follow, let alone when used to compare different months.

It is at this point that words need to give way to illustrations or diagrams. These can take many forms, some of which are interchangeable.

Whichever type of illustration is chosen, they should only be used when they make the point more effectively than words. Care should be taken that they do not themselves confuse, as is often the case when too much information is crammed into one diagram, rather than spread among several.

More confusion is caused by illustrations that have been produced without sufficient thought being given to the component parts. There are many optical illusions of simple figures, which are well known to graphic artists but which might not occur to the report writer. It is easy to create these illusions by assuming that straight lines, circles or squares are easy to draw, and therefore do not need an expensive artist. The problem with many optical illusions is that what is perceived by one person at first glance is different from that which is perceived by another. A blink or slight movement of the page usually shows the alternative picture, but some people are never able to see it.

Figures 2 and 3 show two classic examples of this phenomenon: the

Figure 2. Is it an ornate goblet, or two people face to face?

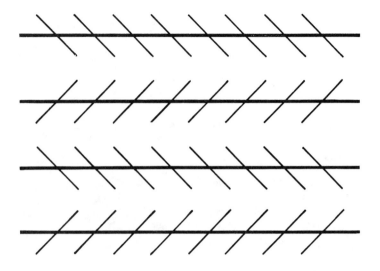

Figure 3. Are the lines parallel, or do they taper?

ornate goblet that transforms into two people face to face, and the series of cross-hatched lines which might be parallel or might taper.

A further sequence of problems comes with pictures which are intended to show comparisons, but fail to do so because of the differences in perception of light and dark shades, or of perspective. Figures 4 and 5 show examples of these. As a general rule it is safer to use graphs or bar charts for comparisons, as most people find it easier to compare two straight lines than two circles, squares or other geometrical figures.

This is why the type of illustration chosen for any given purpose has become a matter of convention. Where such a convention exists it is wisest to stick to it as most readers prefer to be given information in a familiar form.

There are five common methods of showing numerical or statistical data:

(a) tables
(b) graphs
(c) bar charts
(d) pie charts
(e) pictograms.

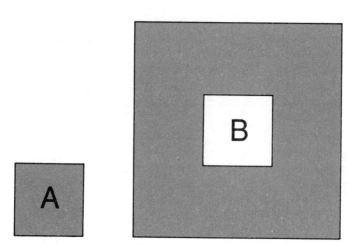

Figure 4. Which is bigger – A or B?

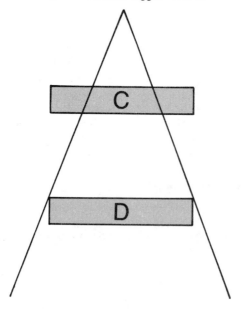

Figure 5. Which is bigger – C or D?

Tables

Tables are made up of columns of figures. Each column is topped by a heading which identifies the figures below. Whenever space permits, these headings should be shown horizontally so they can be read without having to turn the table round. When space is scarce, the headings should be on a clockwise slant, rather than shown by placing the letters from top to bottom (Figure 6a).

Opinions differ on whether headings should be centred in the column or aligned to the left. Where appropriate, the heading should be at the very top, followed by an indication of the status of the figures below. Money is shown by the sterling (£) sign, with pence indicated by use of a decimal point rather than actually being shown in the heading.

Rounding of large figures is shown by an "x" and a sequence of zeros to indicate the magnitude. Zero means "power of 10", so "x000" means the figures in the column are thousands. These are sometimes indicated by using "K" for thousands and "M" for millions.

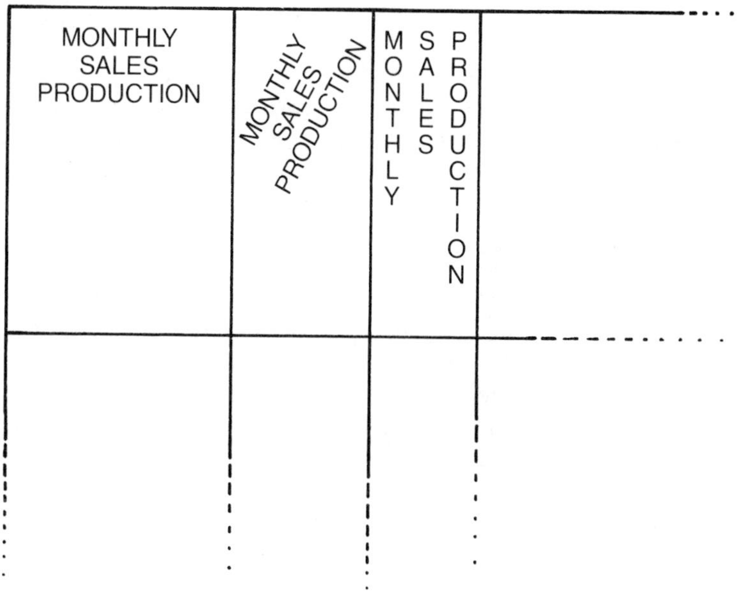

MONTHLY SALES PRODUCTION	MONTHLY SALES PRODUCTION	MONTHLY SALES PRODUCTION	

Figure 6a. Headings should be shown horizontally or on a clockwise slope, not written from top to bottom

Rounding is generally accepted in tables relating to money, but the magnitude of the rounding is dependent on the subject matter. International conglomerates will round the figures in their annual reports to one decimal point of millions, eg $6.7, whereas an internal report comparing the price of widgets will only round up to £s. The grommet pins for the widgets, which cost pennies each, will be shown as £0.07.

Other tables, particularly those relating to scientific, chemical or engineering data will need to show precise figures to several decimal points.

Tables are easier to follow if they are presented in small blocks. For ease of reading, vertical lines should be drawn, if not between every column, then at intervals of no more than six columns. This makes it easier to scan down a column without the eye slipping to the wrong column. Horizontal lines are usually reserved for isolating headings and totals, but spaces every few lines are helpful in long columns. If there is no natural division of data, leaving a space after every three lines breaks the figures up into acceptable chunks. Figure 6b shows a simple table.

Graphs

Graphs are used either to show trends or the relationship between two or more related factors. Examples of the first type can be seen regularly in the business sections of newspapers, showing the progression of inflation or stock market prices. The latter can be found in books on economic history, showing the relationship between industrial production and the birth rate in the early 19th century, or between grain harvests and weather patterns in Russia.

Graphs are easier to read than tables of figures, but they can be misleading, especially when the scale shown in the vertical axis does not start at zero, or when the horizontal scale is compressed or extended. It is not unknown for this to be done deliberately when using two or more graphs to show rival products (see Figure 7).

When drawing graphs it is sensible to use graph paper to assure accuracy of scale. The ideal graph paper to use is the sort that is printed in a shade of grey that does not photocopy, so the end product is not filled with tiny shadowy squares. If grid lines are required, they can be drawn in with a fine pencil or pen.

Bar charts

Bar charts, like graphs, can be used to show trends or variations. They are

MONTHLY WIDGET PRODUCTION											
J	F	M	A	M	J	J	A	S	O	N	D
No. of Machinists											
23	23	22	21	21	21	22	20	23	23	23	22
Daily Widget Production											
361	361	341	315	314	313	330	293	356	361	361	327
Average per Machinist											
16	16	15.5	15	15	15	15	14.5	15.5	16	16	15

Figure 6b. A simple table

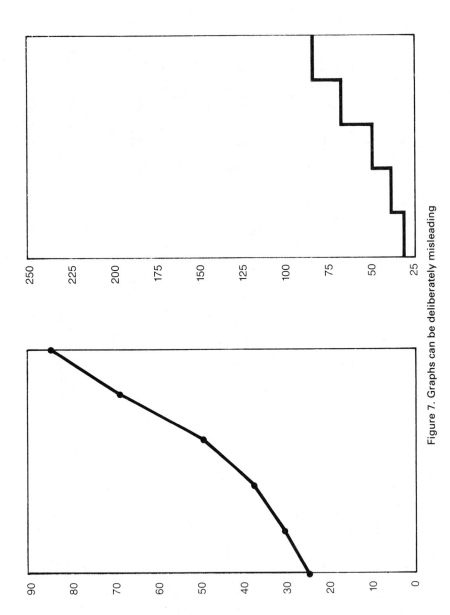

Figure 7. Graphs can be deliberately misleading

frequently used by investment businesses to show the difference in perform-ance between investment products such as unit trusts and the humbler building society deposit. They are clearest when comparing only two items, but can be used for more if the size of the chart and the scope for different shadings or colour printing permits. In general, the more items there are, the better it is to use a series of charts.

The width of the bars should not be varied in an attempt to show more than one aspect in each chart since this only serves to distort the picture. Where the intention is to show an expansion beyond both the trend and the scale of the chart, it is better to "break" the bar with a zig-zag and add a figure to indicate the magnitude.

Pie charts

Pie charts are used to show proportions – literally as slices of a pie. They are popular in financial reports, often being used to show how a local coun-cil divides its income between education, garbage collection and so on.

They are sometimes shown in fanciful forms, such as mortgage figures shown as divisions of the top of a chimney pot complete with television aerial and a tiled roof. Contrary to the expectations of the producers of these drawings, the effect is to trivialise rather than enhance the data. For serious information it is best to stick to simple illustrations.

Pie charts should be drawn as accurately as possible and the actual value of each slice should be shown. Too many slices spoil the visual impact, so if there are many more or less equal slices it is better to use a different type of diagram. Where there are a few big slices and many slices which are too small for the value of each to be shown easily, a "magnifying glass" tech-nique can be used to pull out and enlarge the section containing the small slices (see Figure 8).

Pictograms

These are charts which use pictures instead of numbers. The pictures will be in the form of silhouettes or very simple stylised figures. They are popular with newspapers, which use them to show such things as troop movements, with rows of tanks, aeroplanes and battleships; and with insurance companies who use them to present accident statistics or mortality tables.

Being rather simplistic, pictograms can easily look patronising, and are thus inappropriate for formal business reports. They should not be attempted by anyone other than a professional artist unless the items chosen are available as stencils or transfers (see Figure 9).

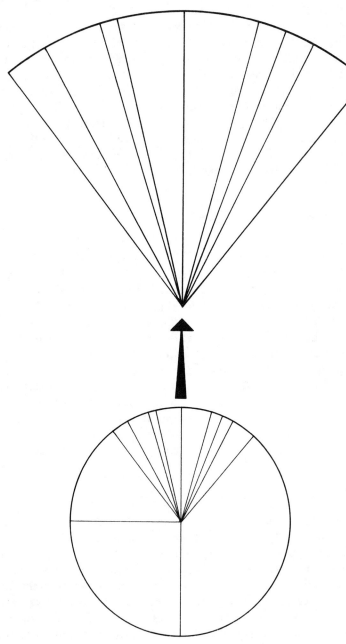

Figure 8. Magnifying glass technique for pie charts

Figure 9. Pictogram showing the military strength of Ruritania

Other Information

Where the information to be conveyed is not numerical there are still conventions as to the form which should be used. Those most commonly seen are:

   (a) flow charts
   (b) genealogical tables
   (c) maps and plans
   (d) line drawings
   (e) photographs.

Flow charts

These charts consist of a series of instructions or questions which are often shown inside boxes which are connected to each other by lines. These boxes are not strictly necessary, but do show at a glance what the chart is for.

Flow charts originated in the computer industry where they are still used by systems analysts to chart the steps needed to perform a task. There are conventions among computer people as to the shape of the box used to show different actions, eg a cylinder is used to indicate use of a disk drive, but for other purposes the shape of the box is less important as long as it is consistent. It is usual to put questions in a different shape of box from other instructions.

The basic principle in flow charting is that only the relevant factors are shown. They are most frequently used to show the steps needed to complete a task or to analyse the cause of a problem.

Instead of writing a sentence full of "if " clauses, the use of a flow chart involves only two options by posing a series of questions that can only be answered "yes" or "no". The skill in writing a good flow chart lies in phrasing each question so that all the "yes" answers flow in one line and all the "no" replies flow in another. This lessens the risk of mistakes by those who are following the chart.

Where a "yes" answer is essential to taking the correct step, "no" replies usually lead round in a circuit of further instructions that go back to the starting point. These circles can end up as a confusing series of concentric circles if care is not taken in the drafting.

The only "rules" relating to flow chart construction are that the flow should be from top to bottom and left to right, and that there should be no crossed lines (see Figure 10).

Genealogical tables

These are traditionally used to show management structures (see Figure 11). They can be shown with the most senior position at the top or on the left side. Where the structure is complex, junior staff can be shown by a number or in a subsidiary table. In some organisations all that is shown is the job title, while others also show the name of the job holder.

Genealogical tables can be used for other purposes, such as shareholding structures or the stages involved in building a complex product such as a car. In other words, anything with a pyramidical structure can be shown in this way.

These tables often need to be dated: where job structures or the names of individuals are shown, this is essential.

Maps and plans

These have already been discussed in Chapter 3 in connection with accident reports, but they are used for many other purposes, such as:

Typewriter Print Faults – identification and correction.

Fault 3 – tops of characters not printed.

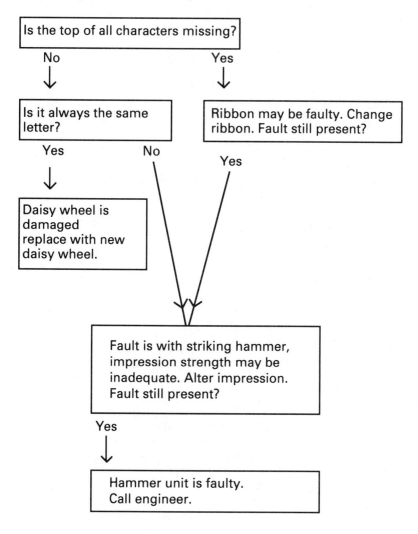

Figure 10. Simple Flow Chart

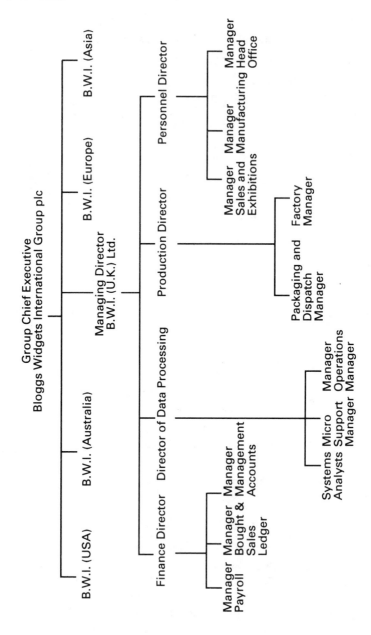

Figure 11. Simple genealogical table of management structure

(a) locating sites of commercial or political significance
(b) indicating demographic details within a country
(c) showing destinations and routes of transport systems
(d) showing variations in terrain
(e) showing reorganisations of floor space.

North should always be shown on maps, even when it seems unnecessary to the writer and both maps and plans should include a statement of the scale, either as a small scale in a corner or as a legend, eg "1cm = 1km".

Depending on what they depict, maps need not necessarily be meticulously drawn so long as what they portray is obvious. The commonest candidates for impressionistic shapes are outlines of countries and continents.

Maps should not be cluttered with too much information. As with pie charts, it is better to use the magnifying glass technique to pull out areas of special interest.

Line drawings

These are most commonly used to show the dimensions of a complex object such as an engine, or to show its component parts. Whatever their purpose, they must be correct and precise and for these reasons can only be drawn by professional technical artists.

Manufacturers may require "orthographic" drawings, which are scale plans of the four main views – top, sides, back and front; or "exploded" drawings of the components making up a complex product. These show each component pulled away from its companions so that each can be seen in the correct relationship, rather than as a set of drawings of each individual part.

"Isometric" drawings show the whole object without perspective, while "perspective" drawings give the layman a better idea of what the object looks like. Where the item exists in reality rather than in a designer's imagination, a photograph may be preferred.

Photographs

Where the report writer wants only to show the readers what something looks like, photographs are probably easier to produce than line drawings. But where the intention is to make some point about the object or place involved, it is often better to use a line drawing which can show only what is relevant and even exaggerate particular aspects to ensure that the point is made.

It takes a very skilled photographer to produce pictures showing specifics, even in a fully equipped studio. When the subject matter is out of doors it can take many hours or even days of waiting for the light conditions to allow the desired photograph to be taken.

There are also technical difficulties attached to reproducing photographs in printed form. It is possible to attach ordinary photographic prints to report pages, but no matter how carefully this is done, it always gives an amateurish impression. The origination of colour photographs for printing is extremely expensive and thus restricted to large print runs.

Although black and white photographs are easier and cheaper to incorporate in a printed document, they actually require more skill on the part of the photographer in order to do the subject justice.

In general, line drawings are better for report illustrations than photographs. This does not mean that the artist has to go to the object, as even the most amateur of photographers can produce a reasonable Polaroid picture for guidance.

Presenting Illustrations

Useful though illustrations are, they should not be added to a report unless there is a good reason for their presence. As with other information, if it does not further the purpose of the report, it should be omitted, no matter how difficult it was to obtain and no matter how attractive it is. Extraneous illustrations only puzzle the reader, who flips back and forth through the pages seeking an explanation and wondering if the printer has missed out the caption.

Location

No illustration is self-explanatory so not only should it be referred to in the text but it should also be placed as close to the relevant portion of the text as is possible, provided that this does not involve dissecting a paragraph. Ideally, the reader should be able to see the illustration while reading the text about it. It is extremely irritating to have to turn pages to find illustrations.

Titles

Even when they are placed immediately adjacent to the text in which they are discussed, all illustrations should still be titled and numbered. The title should be placed at the head or foot of the illustration, not at the side where it could be interpreted as a label for part of the picture rather than the heading for the whole thing.

Numbering

Numbers can be allocated in two ways:

(a) sequentially throughout the report
(b) sequentially throughout each section, with the section number preceding the sequence number, thus Fig. 2.2.

The first method is easier to follow, but organisational convention may preclude its use.

Abbreviations

Abbreviations are a common cause of confusion in reports. This confusion can be avoided by using British Standards unless organisational convention differs. These different conventions are most likely to be encountered in multinational companies and it is sensible in such cases to include a section on abbreviations in the glossary.

One abbreviation that is open to confusion is the presentation of dates. In Britain, 10/12/90 means 10th December 1990. In America it means 12th October. For this reason, columns showing dates should be headed "DD/MM/YY" or "MM/DD/YY" as appropriate. In other situations the month should be written in words. A three letter abbreviation of the month is acceptable in tables or graphs but not in the text of a formal report. In these, the year should always be shown in full.

Care should be taken with single letter abbreviations, as upper and lower case may mean different things. The lower-case letter "m" means "metre", but "M" means "million". There is no need to pluralise abbreviations by adding an "s" at the end. For example, "m" means "metres" as well as "metre". Full stops should not be added to abbreviations unless they occur at the end of a sentence.

Layout

Illustrations should be set within the same margins as the text. This does not mean that they must not be smaller, only that they should not overflow, as this gives the impression that something went wrong at the printer.

Margins serve to create a frame round both text and illustrations which allows the eye to accept the information easily. Empty spaces within illustrations serve the same purpose and where they occur naturally in a graph or other diagram they should be left empty instead of being cluttered up with explanatory words.

Where an illustration occupies a whole page, it may be easier on the eye when presented in landscape format (longer than high) instead of portrait format (higher than long). In this case the bottom of the picture should be on the right, so that the turn required is clockwise, in the same way as column headings.

Physical production

When the report writer has to prepare the diagrams without the assistance of an artist, the main thing to consider is clarity. A fine-nibbed drafting pen should always be used. These pens are designed to draw lines at a constant thickness. Nibs of 0.5mm will suit most diagrams.

Non-artists will want labels in their diagrams to be typed. There are two ways of ensuring they are put in the right place: either write in a very soft pencil that can be typed over and rubbed out or write them on a photocopy of the diagram and give the original to the typist.

Unless the report is to be printed or photocopied in colour, black ink should always be used. When the report is to be photocopied it is worth using the grey printed graph paper which does not photocopy, to give accurate lines and right angles.

Compasses and a protractor should always be used to draw circles and measure angles accurately. Many other shapes are available as stencils from graphic art supply shops.

Copyright

The report writer is responsible for obtaining any necessary permission to use copyright materials. This includes illustrations copied from books or other published documents and may even include photographs taken especially for the report, unless the contract with the photographer specifies otherwise.

Permission to use copyright material is not given in a blanket form, but is valid only for a single specified purpose, unless stated otherwise.

Summary

Words are not always the ideal way to convey information. The use of illustrations can save space and they have more impact than many lines of prose. Illustrations fall naturally into two main types: those used for numerical data and those used for other purposes. In each case, a particular type of illustration is chosen according to convention.

All illustrations should relate to matters discussed in the text and should ideally be located close to that text. They should be numbered and ticked and any abbreviations used in the captions or column headings should be based on British Standards or local conventions.

It is the report writer's responsibility to obtain permission to use copyright material.

Chapter 6
Writing

Once all the data has been collected, sorted, checked and organised into a logical sequence, this set of raw data must be changed into a readable report. In other words, the report writer must start to write.

Even the most experienced of professional writers can find this moment daunting, so the newcomer should not assume that a lack of enthusiasm for putting pen to paper or fingers to keyboard is an indication of failure. Anyone who can write a business letter can write a report. The only difference is a matter of scale and possibly of style.

Style

Style is very difficult to define. To a certain extent it is a matter of readability, but it also encompasses the ability to persuade the reader to share the writer's viewpoint and to allow the writer's personality to be glimpsed. It is the manner of writing that transforms a collection of dull facts into a rounded picture of an event, a situation or a solution to a problem.

Since reports tend to be formal documents, they are usually written in formal language. This can lead to a stilted style from writers who are used to a less formal type of communication. But formality need not be complex. A simple style is the most readable and thus the most satisfactory.

Formality

The actual level of formality required will be dependent on a number of factors:

(a) convention in the organisation
(b) the type of report
(c) status differences between the writer and the readers.

Convention

Although it might be worth discreetly investigating the origin of whatever conventions apply, in general it is not wise to attempt to break with a long-established one. The larger the organisation, the more important it is to have consistency so that readers can easily absorb information in a form that is familiar to them.

Types of report

The more serious the subject matter is, the more appropriate formality becomes. There is no room for frivolity in a report on a serious accident, and the absolute formality of writing in the third party is appropriate in such circumstances. Non-judgemental descriptions should be used in situations where litigation may follow.

On the other hand, if the subject is not a matter of life or death and the organisation itself is one that does not subscribe to formality, a rigidly formal style of writing can seem pompous.

Status differences

A lack of formality in a report written by a junior for the benefit of senior management may be interpreted as impertinent familiarity. The same familiarity in a report written by a superior for the benefit of subordinates may be thought patronising. It is not always easy to achieve the right balance, but there are usually precedents in the form of earlier reports which can be studied.

In general, formality tends to be more wordy than informality. "We think. . ." is informal, "We believe that. . ." is fairly formal, while "It is our belief that. . ." is formal to the point of bordering on the pompous. Some writers go even further and use " The Board of Bloggs Widgets. . ." throughout their report instead of using the friendlier " We".

Pomposity is often a result of a desire to impress by using important sounding words, such as "advise" instead of "tell", "remunerate" instead of "pay", or "ascertain" instead of "find out". These words may be tolerable in a very formal context, but they are merely ludicrous when describing everyday events.

Formal language should always be grammatically correct. A good basic rule when writing is that the written word should be a reflection of the way the writer speaks, but this rule does not apply when formality is needed. Few people today use the correct "to whom . . ." in speech, but this level of correctness must be used in formal writing.

Slang is inappropriate, even though certain examples may be in common usage in a particular industry.

Formal writing does not necessarily have to be in the third person but the inexperienced writer may attempt to use this form in the mistaken belief that it is easier to write. It can be, but there is a pitfall here for the unwary, in that it can become convoluted and extremely tiresome to read.

It may be difficult to define good style and even more difficult to lay down rules on how to achieve it but one thing is indisputable: good style is easy to read.

Grammar

Grammar is a subject that frightens many people, especially those whose education did not include the old discipline of "parsing" a sentence by defining its component parts. Grammar is often defined as "the rules governing the use of language" and it includes the arcane arts of punctuation and spelling as well as sentence construction.

For those who aspire to become good writers, no better advice can be given than to read the quality daily newspapers. Not just the ordinary reporting of daily events, but also the considered essays of regular columnists whose every word is chosen and placed to convey a precise meaning and effect.

For this purpose, the content of their articles and the opinions they express are irrelevant. What matters is the elegance with which those opinions are expressed. Many of them favour very long, multi-punctuated sentences, but this should not put off the less experienced writer.

Punctuation

Perfectly understandable and readable writing need involve no more punctuation than full stops and commas. A comma is used for a short pause, a full stop for a longer pause.

In between commas and full stops are colons (:) and semicolons (;). A semicolon gives a slightly longer pause than a comma and a colon is longer again without being as long as a full stop. Both are the cause of confusion and both can be avoided with some judicious rewording.

Another area of sentence construction that can cause some confusion is the use of two commas to insert something which then makes it look as though the tense is wrong. The rule is that the words between the commas should be seen as an afterthought and should not affect the structure of the basic sentence. If doubt exists, all that is needed is to read the sentence aloud without the matter between the commas.

Sentences and paragraphs

Reading out loud is a good way to check the length of a sentence. If one breath does not last to the end of the sentence it is generally because that sentence is too long. Since that length is generally caused by cramming in too much information, it should be comparatively easy to break it into two or more sentences by separating the information.

Overlong sentences, no matter how elegantly punctuated, are difficult to assimilate, and slow down the process of reading. The average reader should not be expected to cope with sentences of more than 30 words.

Short sentences are easier to read and, from the writer's point of view, easier to control; but too many short sentences in succession are monotonous and soon become annoying. The answer is to vary the length of sentences in each paragraph.

This should not be too difficult, as a paragraph should be constructed in more or less the same way as a sentence. Both should deal with only one chunk of information; a small piece in each sentence and a wider aspect consisting of several sentences in a paragraph. This is known as the "topic" of the paragraph. The usual structure is a short sentence which establishes the topic, followed by other sentences of varying lengths which elaborate on that subject.

Changes of topic from one paragraph to the next allow for longer pauses which make the whole document easier to read.

For this reason, paragraphs themselves should not be too long. It is daunting to be faced with a large unbroken block of text, and usually unnecessary as most topics, and thus paragraphs, can be divided into subtopics.

Readability and clarity

There is a method of measuring the readability of a piece of writing which counts the length of sentences and the complexity of the words themselves. Called "the fog index", it involves:

(a) choosing several samples of 100 words
(b) dividing that number of words by the number of sentences to obtain an average
(c) counting the number of words with three or more syllables (not words starting with capital letters; or with the endings -ed, -es or -ing; or composite words like machine-gun)
(d) adding the answers to (b) and (c) and multiplying by 0.04.

If the answer is less than 10, the writing is easy to read, but if it is greater than 16 it will only be readable by university graduates.

Although many organisations will only consider graduates for positions in management, there are still many senior managers who have not been to university and who have quite small working vocabularies. Whether or not the report writer follows any of the complex rules of grammar and syntax, there is one cardinal rule that should never be broken: write for the reader.

There is more to this than considerations of vocabulary. It is a basic human failing to assume that everyone will respond in the same way to a given situation, or draw the same conclusions from a given set of facts. Report writers are often guilty of this assumption and fail to explain why certain relationships will lead to a particular conclusion. It is the writer's job to make sure that the reader arrives at the proper conclusion.

One way of doing this is to choose examples from areas known to be of particular interest to the readers. Obviously this is easiest when the report is aimed at a small, known, readership, but it should only be attempted if the writer has detailed knowledge of the subject. It does more harm than good to invent examples relating to the chief decision maker's favourite hobby, for it is all too easy to make some crass error through ignorance.

Tightness

This is a term that puzzles many new writers, but it is an aspect of writing that is closely linked to clarity. Writers who are unsure of themselves, or who have not taken the trouble to check their facts, tend to pepper their statements with qualifying words such as "may", "often", or "sometimes". This is known as loose writing.

It is not always possible to be precise, but it is more important in a report than in other forms of writing. Since reports are essentially dealing with facts, it should not be too difficult to pin down vague measurements of occurrence to specific percentages.

It is also a writer's job to say exactly what is meant, not to offer generalities and leave the readers to reach their own conclusions. The English language is one of the most flexible in the world, but it includes many words which have several meanings. Using one of these words inadvertently can make a mockery of what was intended to be a serious statement.

Examples are:

broken down – split up into, or non-functioning because damaged?

single – alone, or unmarried?

This sort of ambiguity can be avoided by a more careful choice of words or it may require more words. Using enough words to make the meaning clear is not the same as being unnecessarily wordy. Some writers use a lot of "padding" words such as "absolutely" or "totally" when the words they have been attached to need no such qualification.

"Final" means the last, so adding "absolutely" to it cannot add any emphasis, any more than "quite" can qualify fatal. Fatal means causing death, and death cannot be qualified: if something is not dead, it is alive. Yet both these expressions are so common that they have become clichés.

Clichés should be avoided (like the plague?) because, like mixed metaphors, they distract the reader's attention from the content of the writing to the quality of the writing. All too often, mixing metaphors comes from the unthinking coupling of clichés.

Examples are:

"I believe they are trying to sell us a pig in a poke as they are as close as a clam about the fuel consumption."

"They're making a real cat's cradle of this with their dog-in-the-manger attitude."

Common mistakes

There are many common mistakes which also distract the reader's attention. These mistakes fall into the following categories:

(a) wrong use of words that sound almost alike
(b) wrong spelling of words that sound alike
(c) wrong spelling of other words
(d) misplaced use of the singular form
(e) confusion over use of singular and plural verb forms
(f) incorrect use of apostrophes.

Wrong use of words that sound almost alike

Here are some of the most common pairs of words which are misused, with their proper meanings:

affect (make a difference)	effect (the result)
authenticate (check)	authorise (allow/permit)
confirm (verify)	conform (comply with custom)
deprecate (state disapproval)	depreciate (reduce value)
disinterested (impartial)	uninterested (bored)
elicit (to draw out)	illicit (unlawful)
ensure (make certain)	insure (guard against loss)
militate (be in conflict)	mitigate (make less severe)
perspective (visual relationships)	prospective (probable future)
rebate (discount)	rebutt (argue)

Wrong spelling of words that sound alike

These fall into two categories:

(a) those which sound alike but mean different things, such as:

forward (in front)	foreword (preface)
formally (in formal manner)	formerly (in the past)
principal (most important)	principle (doctrine)
read-out (computer-produced document)	redoubt (small fort)
re-sort (sort again)	resort (holiday place)
there (location)	their (belongs to them)

(b) those which change spelling when they are used for different parts of speech, such as:

    (i)   a dependant is a person who is dependent on another

    (ii) a licensed victualler is a person who has a licence to sell food and drink

    (iii) to maintain a machine properly, it must have regular maintenance.

Wrong spelling of other words

1. Some words are incorrectly spelt because they are sloppily pronounced when spoken, such as "Pacific" (an ocean) when what is meant is "specific" (of a particular kind); or definate (there is no such word) instead of definite.

2. Words which include both "c" and "s", such as "necessary" or

"occasion" confuse many people as to where the double letter should be.

3. Words which contain "ie" or "ei" also cause confusion. The old chant of "I before E except after C" is only helpful without its second line of "except sometimes!".

In all situations of doubt, the only way to be sure is to consult a dictionary.

Misplaced use of the singular form

Some words which are used only in the plural form, that is with an "s" at the end, are mistakenly used in the singular by dropping the "s". Those most commonly encountered in this form are:

(a) "len", meaning a single lens as opposed to two or more lenses

(b) "good" used to mean a single item of merchandise. "Good", as any dictionary will confirm, is an adjective only. The noun "goods" refers to single or plural merchandise.

Confusion over use of singular and plural verb forms

This usually arises in a sentence where both singular and plural are involved, as in " The use of comparative data is essential when preparing a report." Since "data" is a plural word, surely it should be followed by "are" instead of "is". The question arises from confusion over the subject of the sentence, which in this case is *what* is used, not the plurality of that thing.

If in doubt, the offending phrase should be replaced by something else temporarily and the sentence read aloud: " The use of a herd of elephants *is* essential." The subject of the sentence is "the use", not the things which are being used. For "are" to be the correct verb form, the subject of the original example would have to be the *uses* of comparative data.

Incorrect use of apostrophes

There are only two ways in which an apostrophe can be used correctly:

(a) to indicate that one or more letters have been left out, as in "it's" as a short form of "it is" or "I've" as a short form of "I have"

(b) to indicate possession, as in "Fred's car", which is still a short form of "Fred, his car".

Apostrophes should not be used anywhere else, but often are, incorrectly. For instance, "on it's own" is incorrect, as the "it" cannot possess.

Apostrophes should not be used with plural words, for instance, "fresh egg's for sale".

Jargon and specialised vocabularies

Special care must be taken in choosing words when reports on specialised subjects will be read by a general readership.

The word "jargon" is derogatory, as it refers to technical terms used to exclude the lay person in an "I know something you don't know" version of superiority. This is irritating when the words used have no other use, but can be offensive when the words are in common usage.

For instance, the life assurance industry uses the description "joint life, second death" of a type of policy it sells to married couples for two main reasons: mortgage protection and inheritance tax alleviation. The former is mostly bought by young couples who do not give a thought to mortality, but the latter is sold to many couples in late middle age who can be deeply shocked by the realisation that one of them is going to be widowed. The people who write the brochures are so accustomed to using the term "second death" as a label for a product that it does not occur to them that it is callous.

In situations of this sort it is best to use different words, but where specialised words have to be used they should be explained. If there are many, a glossary should be included. If there are few, each should be explained the first time it is used.

If the report has no other material in footnotes, and if there are no more than half a dozen such words in the report, explanatory footnotes can be used. Otherwise a brief definition should be given in the text, either in brackets or prefaced by "This terms means . . . ' or " This is the process whereby . . ."

The same applies to sets of initials. The first time they are used, they should be in brackets after the full title, eg "Kent County Council (KCC)" after which they can be used without further explanation.

Consistency

Unless a report is quite short, or can be written without breaks, inconsistencies are bound to creep in. Although a sheet of notes can be referred to throughout the writing, this can interrupt the flow, in which case it is better to leave such niceties for the revision stage.

Many professional writers firmly believe that it does not matter if the first draft is disjointed. The important thing is to get something on paper. It can always be sorted out later at the revision stage. It should be noted from this that professional writers do not think they can get away without revising their work!

There are several stages to revision, ranging from the simple to the compound:

(a) grammatical checking
(b) consistency checking
(c) repetition and contradiction
(d) semantics
(e) balance
(f) cross-referencing
(g) numbering systems.

Unless the report is very short, each of these stages should be treated as a separate exercise.

Grammatical checking

This should never be omitted, no matter how experienced or how grammatically confident the writer may be. The purpose of grammar is to make sense of what is written and what may have seemed sensible after a good lunch or late at night might not do so several days later.

Grammatical checking should be done on a paragraph basis, looking for errors of punctuation, sentence construction and spelling.

Consistency checking

This should cover the next level up from the grammatical checking of each paragraph, to ensure that nothing changes between paragraphs or even pages. The person used, the tense, the pronouns, and even the longer descriptions of people, places or events should not change, eg if a property is referred to as " No. 3, The Grove" at the beginning of the report, it should not change to "House A" half-way through.

This is most important with names and titles, which must remain in the same form throughout the report. "The Spear Lance and Sword

Company" may be abbreviated to "SLS" but should not be called by its full name in some places and "Spears" in others. The same applies to product names, especially where there have been several models with the same name. Spears' "Goliath mark 2" lance may be very much better than the mark 1 version and those who are only familiar with the inferior version will conclude that the report writer who sings the praises of the "Goliath" lance is a fool.

Where there is any possibility of words having alternative spellings, they must be checked to ensure that only one version has been used.

Checking all these areas is particularly important if more than one writer has contributed to the report, and especially if the writers do not come from the same side of the Atlantic. Not only spelling, but many other areas of language usage are different, ranging from frequency of prepositions, the placing of hyphens and even some verb forms. (In England, the past tense of "dive" is "dived"; in America it is "dove".)

Repetition and contradiction

This applies on both the large scale and the small.

On the large scale, especially when there have been long pauses between the writing of various sections, it is quite common for arguments or chunks of information to be repeated. Nor is it uncommon for a writer to get so carried away with the details of opposing viewpoints that the relationship between the two extremes gets missed out. If, as a result of late information, the writer's viewpoint or interpretation of the facts has changed, the earlier arguments will have to be amended.

On a smaller scale, checking for repetition consists of searching for and eliminating excessive use of certain words and phrases. Just as the audience listening to a bad speaker stop listening to the speech and devote their attention to counting the number of times a favourite word is used, overuse of such a word in a report can make the rest of the words fade into insignificance. It is particularly noticeable if more than two successive paragraphs start with the same phrase.

Semantics

Just as those who are uncertain of the spelling of a word should check it in a dictionary, so too should those who are not absolutely certain of a word's meaning. This is most important when the repetition check has lead to various words being changed for variety.

This is also the time to weed out the vague words like "recently" instead of "during May"; the loaded words like "alien" instead of "foreign"; the pompous words like "cogitate" instead of "think" and the padding words like "of all" following "first".

Balance

In general, the sections of the main body of the report should be of a length relative to their importance. In many cases, over-elaboration can be consigned to an appendix, while large amounts of essential data can be condensed into chunks.

The most important part may have been so boring that it has been skimped, or an aspect that is of minor importance to the whole may have been over-reported because it is a subject dear to the writer's heart. Either of these imbalances can affect the whole of the report and thus its effectiveness.

Cross-referencing

Whatever system of cross-referencing has been used, it should be checked to make sure that it works by actually looking for the other half of each reference and ensuring that it has its own reference indicator.

Numbering systems

In an organisation where numbering systems are a matter of convention, this check should involve little more than making sure that paragraph 4b follows 4a and is itself followed by 4c or 5.

In organisations where such things are left to each writer, or where several writers have worked on the report, it is important to check that the notation is both logical and consistent.

There are three basic types of numbering system:

(a) strict paragraph numbering
(b) decimal notation or alpha notation
(c) mixed systems.

Strict paragraph numbering

This is the system used for government reports. Each paragraph has a sequential number, starting with 1 and carrying on to 987 or whatever.

The advantage of this system is that any paragraph can easily be identified and located and thus can be discussed at meetings or on the telephone.

The disadvantage is that it gives no indication of the importance of paragraphs or section divisions.

Decimal or alpha notation

This system is simple in its concept, but can become ridiculous if many levels of subdivision are needed.

1. Major headings and sections are given a single arabic number.

1.1 The first level of subdivision has another single arabic number after a decimal point.

1.1.1 Each successive subdivision has another decimal point.

1.1.1.1 Four subdivisions begins to be cumbersome and any more are risible.

The alpha version often uses alternative upper- and lower-case letters.

Mixed systems

These use a combination of alpha and numeric figures and may use roman as well as arabic numerals. With a limited number of subdivisions, this system is the easiest to follow, usually going from upper-case alpha to arabic numeric then lower-case alpha and finally roman numeric. It is beyond that stage that difficulties set in.

Although possibly the most widely used system, it is the one that needs the most careful checking for consistency.

Summary

Good style is what makes a piece of writing easy to read. Many reports need to be written in a formal way and care should be taken that formality does not become pomposity.

Good grammar is important and this includes punctuation and sentence construction. Clarity is essential and can be achieved by careful choice of words.

There are many common mistakes which distract the reader's attention from the content of the report. If in doubt, a dictionary should be used. When the writing stage is finished the work should be carefully revised to eliminate errors and inconsistencies. This is particularly important when several writers have contributed.

Chapter 7
Conclusions and Recommendations

Most senior managers and other decision makers want to be presented with a simple decision: do we do it or don't we? The "it" being a firm recommendation from someone who has weighed all the facts before making the proposal.

Obviously if a large sum of money is involved, the facts may be double-checked by an expert, but in general the person who wrote the report is considered to be the best person to draw conclusions and make recommendations.

The Summary

The longer the report, the more important it becomes to summarise its contents before stating conclusions. Although the summary is usually presented at the beginning of the report it cannot be written until the main body is finished. It is at this point that the value of the final stages of revisions, particularly those relating to balance, become apparent.

Writing the summary is an important part of writing reports and adequate time should be allowed to do a thorough job. Although the finished summary should ideally occupy no more than two pages, it must still consist of balanced paragraphs and be laid out so that it is easy to read.

In its simplest form the summary needs no more than three paragraphs:

1. A brief statement of the purpose of the report and the terms of reference. In a scientific report a mention of any relevant limitations may be included.
2. A summary of the main body of the report, broken up into sentences that can be linked to the headings used in the report itself.
3. A final paragraph covering the conclusions and recommendations. Although this paragraph should not be too wordy it must be sufficiently detailed for the readers to follow the logic that has lead to the conclusions.

Where a more complex report is involved, the summary can be extended by adding more paragraphs about the main body, or dealing with the conclusions and recommendations separately.

The best way to tackle the writing of the summary is to start by ignoring the "two pages only" restriction and writing as long a summary, within reason, as seems necessary to cover all the material. Then go through it and weed out anything which is not essential to understanding. It is always easier to cut out excess material than to add essentials later.

The final step is to apply the technique used by journalists working to a wordage limit. This involves examining each sentence to see if any individual words can be omitted or phrases reworded to make them shorter. "We believe that" becomes "we think", or "we are now in a position to unveil" becomes "we can show".

When deciding what can be cut out or reworded, it is important to remember that the summary should stand on its own. In many instances it will be circulated without the rest of the report, often to senior people who have no particular interest in the subject but who feel they should be kept informed. It is these people who tend to get hold of the wrong end of the stick, so the summary must be as balanced as the whole of the report and should not omit anything which is essential to the logic of the conclusions. If any of the proposals involve urgent action, this fact must be clearly shown in the summary as well as in the recommendation section.

Since it should stand on its own, the summary must bear the title of the report, any relevant reference codes, an indication of its confidentiality and the date and report writer's name.

Conclusions

Just as the summary should start by stating the purpose of the report, so should the conclusions. This is not needless repetition but a necessary reminder to the reader who will otherwise have to flip back to the beginning of the report to check.

Where the purpose of the report is simple it need only be stated briefly at the beginning of this section, but where the purpose is complex it may be necessary to restate each part as a preamble to that part of the conclusions. This can be done by:

(a) setting the whole purpose out as a series of numbered parts, and then using the same numbering system to set out the conclusions
(b) referring to each part of the purpose as a "given".

Numbered parts

This method is most appropriate for formal reports where the whole of the report is presented in this format. If possible, the numbers used should correspond with the relevant part of the main body of the report. If not, it is advisable to use a different numbering system, as otherwise the reader can become confused at point 2(a) in the conclusions referring to 3(a) in the main body.

"Givens"

This expression reflects the actual words used in this method: "Given that the purpose of this report . . .". It can be used again: "and given that the investigation showed . . ., I conclude that . . .".

It is an acceptable form for both formal and informal reports.

Whichever method is used to break the purpose into parts, the next part of each conclusion is to refer briefly to the evidence which supports the conclusion that follows. It is not necessary to repeat in detail all the evidence or arguments already reported, only to mention the salient points in an order which shows the logic that has led to the conclusion.

It is likely that the evidence will not only be in one section, but scattered throughout the main body. By the very nature of reports, the findings are unlikely to occur in a simple linear fashion and for this reason the conclusions section should be carefully cross-referenced.

The evidence used to arrive at the conclusions should all be in the main body. If it is not, it must be added at the appropriate point, not introduced for the first time in this section. Conclusions can only be drawn after all the evidence has been examined.

The conclusions themselves should not be qualified in any way. If it seems necessary that they should, it can only be because the evidence provided is insufficient. This may be due to sloppy research; or it may be that the situation is one where only time will provide sufficient evidence to arrive at a definite conclusion, in which case all that can be done is to state that the investigation proved inconclusive and recommend that further research should be undertaken.

Conclusions are also known as findings.

Recommendations

Recommendations naturally follow from conclusions and they should not be omitted. Even if the conclusion is that nothing is wrong, it should be recommended that no action should be taken.

It is not always necessary to put the recommendations in a separate section. Even where the conclusions are multiple, the recommendation need not necessarily be any more than one simple statement: that one sort of car should be bought or that head office should be moved to a particular location.

However, where there are multiple recommendations, they should be summarised separately even if they have been made elsewhere. This is not unusual and is common practice in reports on public enquiries. The word "recommended" is emphasised by underlining or italic print throughout the report and all the recommendations are then repeated in a "Summary of Findings and Recommendations".

Recommendations, like conclusions, should be unqualified. This section is no place for a sequence of "if " statements. They should be achievable and for this reason, as well as political tact, it may be necessary to recommend that "efforts should be made" or "a high priority should be given".

Such woolly statements are only possible when no dire consequences will result from failure to act. Where legal requirements or considerations of safety are concerned, recommendations can only be for specific action to be carried out by a specified time.

As a general principle, recommendations should include a time-scale for completion. Multiple recommendations should be listed in order of importance and each segment should include a completion date. It is perfectly reasonable to make one sweeping recommendation, such as "Head Office should be moved to Melton Mowbray, with the move completed by November 1994" and then to continue "In order to achieve this, it will be necessary to:

(a) appoint architects by 31.3.92
(b) brief Public Relations agency by 31.12.93
(c) draw up staff relocation, redundancy and recruitment plans for operation commencing 31.3.94
(d) appoint and brief removal firm by 31.7.94
(e) finalise details for opening ceremony by 31.8.94.

Wherever possible and tactful, the writer should state not only what should be done and when it should be completed, but indicate who should do it. This may not be the obvious people, and where this applies, the reasons should be given. These reasons should not be over elaborated: suggestions for departure from tradition will inevitably lead to discussions and the writer should keep something in reserve for this time.

The writer should never forget the possibility of being called to meetings to justify or elaborate on the recommendations. Recommendations may be put into the third party by stating "It is recommended that . . . " but they are not a product of nature. Someone has to make them. Occasionally it will be an outsider, such as the local fire officer, who has recommended that certain steps be taken, but in general it is the writer who has the responsibility for stating "I recommend".

This is one of the principle reasons for signing a report: that signature is an acceptance of responsibility. In some organisations it is the practice for the report writer's superior to sign the report as well, thus adding a higher level of responsibility as well as approval.

Objectivity

Given that the report writer, or some other named person, has to take responsibility for the recommendations it is very difficult to avoid the implication that they are subjective. Indeed, to a certain extent they cannot be truly objective, for the writer will inevitably have used personal criteria in selecting which facts and opinions are relevant to achieving the stated purpose.

Many writers resort to the impersonal form in an attempt to introduce objectivity. Unless the rest of the report has been written in this form, it should not be introduced for this section.

Summary

A brief summary should be written after the main body of the report, which should be capable of standing on its own. Reports should finish with conclusions and recommendations. These may be together in one section or separately in two sections.

Both the summary and the conclusions section should commence with a restatement of the purpose of the report. Both conclusions and recommendations should be unqualified, and both should be related to the relevant portions of the main report.

The writer must be prepared to accept responsibility for the recommendations by signing the report.

Chapter 8
Production

After all the writing is completed, there is still a little work to be done to prepare the manuscript for typing. Even the most experienced secretary needs to be told how the typescript should be presented.

Good layout is essential if the report is to have the desired impact on its readers. It would be a pity, after all the work that has gone into preparing the report, if it receives a lukewarm reception because its physical appearance is mediocre.

Typing Instructions

To ensure that no mistakes can be made, a list of typing instructions should be compiled on a separate sheet. This should include:

(a) presentation of titles and headings
(b) symbols to be used
(c) spacing and margins
(d) justification of lines and paragraphs
(e) typeface
(f) page numbering
(g) number of copies required
(h) completion deadline.

Titles and headings

The title must stand out. It should be centred in its own space on the page, with nothing close to distract the reader's eye. If possible, it should be in a different typeface to the rest of the report, but at the very least it should be in block capitals. Emphasis can be added by using bold type and underlining.

Section headings should also stand out, but not quite as strongly as the main title. Subheadings should be another degree of magnitude less, so if the main title is in bold block capitals underlined, section headings should omit either the underlining or the emboldening. Subheadings should omit the other, or could be in lower case underlined or bold.

Spacing and margins

There should be good spacing between sections and, as with the magnitude of the headings, these spaces should be greater between sections than between subsections. Short blocks of text are inviting to read but long unbroken sections are daunting.

Spacing between ordinary lines of text should be consistent throughout. While double spacing is required by publishers, it is excessive in reports. 1.5 spacing is usually sufficient.

Margins should also be reasonably wide without leaving so much space that the text looks cramped in the middle of the page. The type of binding to be used should be considered when setting the margins.

Symbols

Where symbols are used they should not only be consistent throughout but should, wherever possible, be those which are generally accepted. Dots are used to indicate parts omitted from quotations, with three dots meaning less than a sentence and six dots meaning at least a whole sentence. Where the writer has had to insert an explanation into a quotation, for instance to explain who "he" is, this insertion should be in square brackets, thus [ ]. This is particularly important where figures are concerned, as ordinary brackets signify a deficit.

Some writers use italics for quotations. This is only acceptable for brief quotations and where there are few of them. Excessive use of italics is distracting to the eye and gives a restless feel to the text.

Where there is some doubt as to the truth of a quoted statement, or where there is an apparent misspelling, the word "sic", which means "as it is written", should be added in brackets immediately after the dubious item.

Justification

This should cover whether all the type should be left "ragged" or justified to the right-hand margin, and also whether paragraphs should be indented or blocked. The modern tendency is for paragraphs to be blocked and separated by a line space.

Typeface

With modern daisy-wheel typewriters or word processing packages on small computers, changing the typeface is quick and easy. Daisy-wheels are merely lifted out and a new one dropped in, while word processing packages using laser printers can change font with three or four key strokes. Some only show one typeface on the screen, but others offer **WYSIWYG** (what you see is what you get) which means the writer can see the report in various fonts before making a final choice.

Page numbering

The pages of any document more than two pages long should be numbered. To a certain extent the location of the number is a matter of personal choice or organisational convention. However, some thought has to be given to the matter of binding and whether the report is to be produced single or double sided.

If it is to be bound and single sided, numbers in left-hand corners are inadvisable as they will be difficult to see. If it is to be double sided, neither corner is advisable, as the numbering will have to be delayed until the final version and then put on alternate left and right corners.

The best place is the centre of the page. The top is probably best as it allows easy reference when looking for a specific page.

Pages should be numbered as soon as they are typed, to avoid losing the sequence if they are dropped. For this reason, manuscript pages should also be numbered. The location of illustrations must be clearly indicated, as they will have to be included in the numbering sequence.

The title page should not be numbered. The contents list is not usually numbered. The summary is best numbered in roman numerals as it may be removed from the report to take on a life of its own.

Most word processing packages have an automatic page numbering facility.

Desktop publishing

These computer programs are easily obtainable and are reasonably cheap. They let the writer see the layout of the report on a screen before it is printed, allow pages to be moved about, and offer many variations on the theme of text enhancement. Some versions also offer graphics facilities, which at the very least can rapidly produce accurately drawn graphs and charts. Some offer colour printing, but this requires a more expensive printer.

Checking

The writer must check the typescript when it is returned. If deadlines permit, at least two days should elapse between writing the manuscript and checking the typescript. This allows the writer to forget the actual words used, and thus to look properly at what has been typed instead of assuming that each phrase is as it was written. For this reason, although the writer should do the first check, a third party should also check it for incongruities the writer might have missed. Another reason for using a third party is that the writer often gets carried away by the brilliance of the writing and just reads on through the typescript instead of actually checking it.

Long sequences of figures should be checked by two people, one reading from the manuscript while the other checks the typescript. If assistance is not available, each set of figures should be totalled on a calculator, first on the manuscript then on the typescript. If the two totals agree, there is no need to check the accuracy of the typed figures, but the eye should still be run down each column in case any of the figures is out of alignment.

Everything must be checked. Errors are just as likely to occur in the title page, contents list or diagram captions as in the main text. Particular care must be taken to check names. At the least irritation and at the worst mortal offence is caused by carelessness over people's and companies' names.

Such carelessness casts doubt on the value of the rest of the report. The assumption is always that it is the writer who is sloppy or ignorant and thus unprofessional, rather than the typist.

It is surprising how often simple typing errors serve to reverse the sense of important statements by the omission or alteration of one letter: "There is now concern . . ." becomes "There is no concern . . .". Unfortunately, both are real words and word processor spell-checking programs will ignore them. This proves that spell chequers are knot infallible! When accuracy is essential, nothing beats the human eye.

When reports are reproduced by any method other than photocopying the typescript, they will have to be proof-read before the final print run. This applies even if they have been set by computer from a word processor disk, as dust, power surges or machine faults can all corrupt electronically held data.

Reproduction

Printing

Unless the style of printing is a matter of organisational convention, or the writer is sufficiently expert to give precise instructions, all aspects should be discussed with the printer. These discussions should cover:

(a) binding
(b) typeface
(c) main text colour
(d) other colours
(e) paper quality, finish and colour.

Binding

Although binding is the last in the sequence of processes, the choice of binding must come first, as it affects page layout and print sequencing.

Ideally, all reports should open to lie flat. It is annoying to have to hold a book or document open when its binding will not allow it to open up completely without disintegrating. However, the practicalities of most report production are that they are printed or photocopied and bound in-house. In this situation, the binding tends to be of a type that captures a portion of the edge of the paper. Margins must be wide enough to allow for this, or text and figures may disappear into the binding.

Available binding methods are:

(a) full book-type binding, with sewn pages and hard covers
(b) "perfect" binding, where the back edges of the pages are trimmed and glued before a soft cover is added. This method is less robust and may not be suitable for more than 100 pages or for glossy paper
(c) booklet binding with sewn or stapled centres (known as saddle-stitching)

(d) spiral or ring bindings. Although bulky, these are probably the most satisfactory for large reports as they look professional and allow the pages to open flat

(e) plastic combs. This is a reasonably cheap process which allows the pages to open flat. The combs are available in various colours, and can themselves carry simple printed titles

(f) slide binders. These are cheap and presentable, but do not allow the pages to open flat. They will take up to 25 pages

(g) staples. These are very cheap but only suitable for internal reports. They allow the corners to fray and crease, and even the deep staples will not hold more than 25 pages

(h) treasury tags. These are very cheap and have an old-fashioned image. If loose enough to allow the pages to open flat they soon tear away from the holes

(i) paper clips – acceptable for internal reports of up to six pages

(j) pins – will only hold three or four pages, are a nuisance to handle and tend to draw blood, so are not a good idea.

Wherever possible, bound reports should have a cover, even if it is no more than a sheet of clear plastic.

Typeface

A typeface that is clear and easy to read should be chosen. A report that is to be reproduced by the expensive method of printing is always intended for a large readership. This inevitably means that a certain percentage of the readers will have difficulty in reading fancy typefaces like Gothic, or anything smaller than 12 point.

Main text colour

Nothing is as easy to read as black print on white paper. Blues or greys are unnecessarily fanciful, and can be very difficult to read in poor light or when printed on tinted paper.

All text should be printed in the same colour. The only opportunity for coloured text is as captions for illustrations in some types of informal report.

It should be remembered that reports are often read when travelling, where good light is not always available.

Other colours

Absolutely accurate colour reproduction is a very expensive process and only worth considering for large print runs. If it is not essential to the integrity of the report, it is preferable to take the printer's advice on the use of colour.

Wherever possible, the use of red and green should be avoided, as these are the two colours which cannot be distinguished by the colour-blind, who see both as grey. This condition is very common and thus should not be overlooked.

Choice of paper

White paper is the cheapest and, for most purposes, the best choice. If colours are used, they should not be so dark that it is difficult to read the printing.

Long and complex reports can benefit from different colours for different sections, but there should be a discernible logic in the choice of colours. If appendices are specific to certain sections, they should be in the same colour as the section to which they relate. A cheaper alternative to different colours for each section is to separate the sections with one sheet of coloured paper.

The quality and finish of the paper is important, not only to the perceived value and impact of the report, but to its physical longevity.

Good matt finish bond paper is the most commonly used for all purposes and thus the cheapest. The actual thickness or "weight" is usually a matter of organisational choice but a good general principle is to use the best that the budget allows.

Gloss finish (or art) paper is more expensive, not only because of the processes involved in its manufacture but also because it is less commonly used than matt finish. It is not always easy to read, especially in artificial light, and some types of binding glue do not stick to it properly.

However, gloss paper is generally more robust and resistant to soiling than matt varieties.

Photocopying

Photocopying is an acceptable method of reproducing internal reports.

The average office photocopier, assuming that it is properly maintained, will give good copies of black type and diagrams on various colours of paper. Ordinary black and white copiers will produce murky results from coloured diagrams, so thought must be given to differentiation of shading in graphs and charts.

Organisations with reprographics departments will have more sophisticated machines and it is worth consulting the machine operator to find out what facilities are available. Some even have colour copiers, or these can be found in commercial print shops.

Laser copiers give very high-quality reproduction of colour photographs from prints or transparencies, but at the time of writing can only do so on one side of the paper.

Summary

Manuscripts must be prepared carefully for typing, with clear instructions on layout. Modern word processing packages allow flexibility but spell-check programs should not be considered an adequate substitute for proper checking of the typescript.

Whether printed or photocopied, various aspects of production should be considered and discussed with the printers. These include binding and choice of paper, typeface and colour.

Chapter 9
Distribution and Presentation

Early Drafts

A high proportion of reports, especially those which are complex, need to go through several drafts before the final version can be signed off and distributed. The early drafts have to be circulated to various interested parties for comments and suggestions which then have to be incorporated in the final version.

Example
A report on setting up a retirement bonus scheme for self-employed life assurance sales personnel.
Draft One consisted of outlines of the areas within the writer's own knowledge, and was circulated to:

(a) the management accountant for comments on accruals and accounting techniques
(b) the commissions department who would have to provide staff to run the scheme
(c) the company's tax expert for comments on tax implications for the company and the recipients
(d) the legal department for comments on how the scheme would affect the sales forces contracts

(e)   the actuarial department, who would have to provide calculations of embedded value of policies sold by the recipients

(f)   the sales management team

(g)   a selected group of long-serving sales personnel.

Draft Two incorporated the comments and suggestions of all the above and offered some tentative recommendations on how to deal with various aspects. It was circulated to all the parties listed above for further comments.

Draft Three was considerably refined and included some specific recommendations. It was circulated to:

(a)   the sales management team

(b)   the group of sales personnel

(c)   the executive committee for discussion and decision at a board meeting.

Draft Four was the final version, giving full details of the agreed scheme. It was circulated to all the parties listed above and the entire sales force, and was incorporated in the documentation given to all future sales recruits.

All of this takes time and requires tactful control. The more people who are involved, the greater the necessity for documentary control mechanisms.

With a very large circulation list, the computer-literate might choose electronic methods, but otherwise a pro forma sheet should be devised. This will need to list all the recipients of each draft, with dates of dispatch, return deadline and actual return. A safety factor of several days should be built into return dates.

As each copy of the draft comes back, it should be checked to ensure it is complete and a note made of which sections bear comments that need following up or require rewriting.

Each person on the circulation list should receive a full copy, which should be returned to the person controlling the circulation. This avoids delays and also the risk of the reports being broken up by people taking out the sections that interest them before passing the rest on.

Ideally each copy should be numbered and show how many copies are in circulation, eg "6 of 24". People who are not on the circulation list who want to see a copy should be referred to the circulation controller rather than be allowed to take their own copies.

In some organisations it may be necessary to exercise tact when allocating numbered copies to different levels of management. Circulation lists in alphabetical order and allocation of numbers from the top down should eliminate any nonsense about seniority.

Later drafts

Any alterations to the original version mean that the entire report will have to be revised again to check for contradiction, illogicality, consistency and balance. Only the portions that have been altered need proof-reading.

It is particularly important to check for changes of style if large passages written by other people have to be inserted. It may be preferable to put these in the appendices or at the end of the section over the contributor's signature. Where the contributor holds high rank it may be preferable to both parties to insert the contribution as a foreword, especially if it is made on the premise "I'm in charge so I must make my mark".

The accompanying memo

Depending on the degree of formality in the organisation, this may not need to say any more than "Here is the first draft of the report I mentioned to you on the telephone. Please let me have it back with your comments by the 7th".

Where outsiders are concerned, this memo (or letter) may need to explain why the recipient has been chosen, which sections are involved, and the nature of the desired contribution. It will also have to cover the nature of acknowledgements and may need to enquire about a fee.

Confidentiality

There are four main reasons for confidentiality:

(a) commercial competition
(b) political expediency
(c) tact
(d) protection of sources.

Commercial competition

This covers all the aspects of business confidentiality, from keeping a new product under wraps until launch day to guarding against industrial espionage. Any business which leads in its field must constantly be on its guard against leaks of information which could benefit competitors. Even a report assessing new manufacturing machinery could benefit competitors, and whilst they might not be prepared to go so far as actively to seek such information, idle chat in a pub by a photocopier operator could filter through.

Political expediency

This covers aspects from the major, such as tentative plans for closing a factory, to the minor, such as the imminent redundancy of an individual.

At both ends of the scale there is scope for damage if the news gets out before any necessary safeguards are organised. The possibility of a factory closure could lead to industrial action, while the redundant individual may have time to wreak spiteful damage before the axe falls.

Tact

This covers areas such as the imminent appointment of a director, who will want to time the news of the change at the most propitious time.

Where senior personnel of publicly quoted companies are concerned, news of departures and arrivals may be designated "price sensitive" and thus "insider information".

Protection of sources

This is less a matter of restricting circulation than a need to exercise great care in the wording of text and choice of illustrations.

While the general reader will not be able to identify products, companies or peripheral bodies such as professional firms by careless reference to a date of introduction or a factory location, people within the same industry or peripheral professions will easily work out what should have been kept secure.

Retaining confidentiality

In extreme cases it may be necessary for the writer, or a trusted aide, to take the typescript to a print shop for reproduction, and then to deliver all copies to the recipients personally and obtain receipts.

Early drafts, manuscripts, notes and research material will have to be kept locked away until they can be personally shredded. In establishments where they take this sort of thing seriously, even the carbon paper and typewriter ribbons are shredded daily. Computer files must be password protected, and disks should not be left lying around.

All of this care can be wasted if people then leave reports in cars, or read them on trains where fellow travellers can look over their shoulders. It should not be forgotten that many people consider the art of reading upside-down to be a necessity for modern business life.

Presentation to Meetings

Whilst all written documents should stand on their own, some individuals and organisations like to have a personal presentation with an opportunity for questions and discussions.

There is little difference between presenting a report and any other sort of business presentation, except that copies of the report should be circulated in advance. The writer should read through the report as many times as necessary to ensure complete familiarity before making the presentation. If there are any areas where additional expertise may be needed for expansion or questions, the experts should be organised and briefed.

All the illustrations should be put on to slides or whatever medium is necessary for the available projection equipment. For less formal presentations where a flip-chart will be used, this will have to be prepared, either completely or in the form of reference points which make it easy to draw freehand at the appropriate time in the presentation.

Summary

Many reports have to be circulated in draft form for comments before the final version is prepared. These drafts should be controlled and a return date set. Any resulting alterations mean complete revision is needed.

Confidentiality may involve rigid security, as breaches could have serious effects.

Some reports have to be presented at meetings, where the presenter will need visual aids and must expect to receive questions.

Index